SPEECHES

FROM THE

CROWD

Kerry Coast

For Ramsey

Electromagnetic Print 2018

Cover photo by Brian Hayden

Produced in Sto:lo and St'át'imc Territories

Catalogued with Library and Archives Canada
- without prejudice -

Coast, Kerry
Speeches From The Crowd

ISBN - 978-1985301849

www.electromagneticprint.com

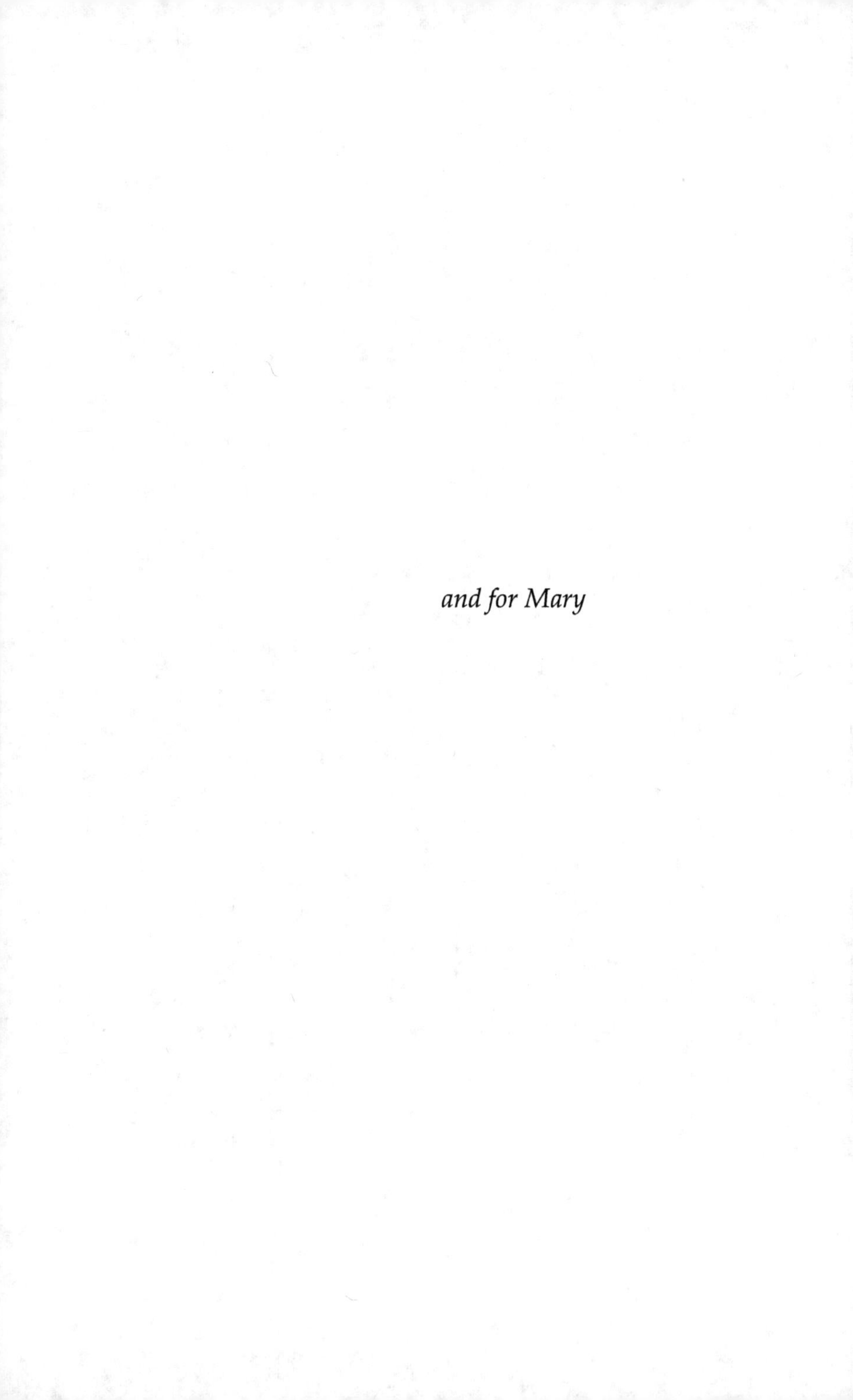

and for Mary

CONTENTS

Speeches

Just among the crowd

speeches

POVERTY FATIGUE

As I wrestled with the extensive demands of single-parenthood: the identity crisis of being both good and bad cop – and everything else – to a small child; the sense of being shut-in like someone under house arrest – their assigned duty the nurture of that child; the pileup of favours from friends and family in getting said child from A to B and the lack of time and energy to repay them; the required dereliction of duty involved with going to work and leaving a sick child at home – or taking a sick child to work – or staying at home with a sick child while work reconsidered my employment; I began to wonder if there isn't something more to this mess than being personally inadequate.

I realized there is. It is poverty. Inescapable, immitigable, irrefutable poverty. And poverty is increasing 'round here. And I'm watching poverty diminish the human capital available to society, if this is a society anymore. And the more privileged sections of society have leaned so far into systems of maintaining economic discrepancy among citizens that their manufactured gap is growing faster than most will admit.

There is a reality to the way people in poverty live, and to what the reality of prolonged poverty does to a person. It may seem unlikely in its unpleasantness. There is a disintegration of the identity of those who live in poverty while they are surrounded with the capital-consciousness of car commercials and faceless offers to re-mortgage houses. They don't have a house and it's a long time since their car was in a commercial. They don't see themselves the way they feel they are supposed to be seen. There is also a gush of statistical explanation for these people, and dismissal, while the same statistic-generating institutions continue to train the upcoming middle class in the ways and world views of disparity and enthusiastically monitored charity.

Maintaining the poor, as they are, is a double-digits of billions of dollars industry which, if reconfigured and reassigned, might very effectively displace the whole constructed role that "the poor" now play in maintaining an intrinsically motivating sense of desperation among the mass work force which dangles just a rung or two up the same economic rope ladder. Part of that reassignment might even fund education on basic human values; societal structures; what social capital is.

Recently some troubled soul has augmented the intellectual commons that is Wikipedia by declaring "poverty fatigue" belongs to "front line workers." They get sick of trying to help poor people solve their unsolvable problems; sick of the dirty, disempowered, impossible choices that are made by the folks they are meant to assist by their government jobs – in whatever way that is – to keep the industrial machine lubed and the powerless cycling through it, alive, in a disposable work force, driving down wages and labour standards. To the poor themselves, Wikipedia allows "decision fatigue."

But poor people don't get to have decisions, and that's the trouble. The poor have dilemmas backed by

ultimatums. People with resources get to make decisions: shall I shop here, or there? How shall I spend my
$50 bonus? Where will I go this Saturday night? Should
I call my mother, or can it wait another week before I
am really past due?

People living under the ugly thumb of poverty
cannot make decisions about where to shop: the store is
in walking distance, or it offers the absolute cheapest
prices and warrants a bus ride. Those in poverty often
try to imagine that $50 is not so hard to get: they must
be able to come up with $50 somehow, since other peo-
ple seem to do so. Maybe they will find a red bill on the
street, or maybe the bank machine will spit one out in
place of a twenty – it has happened.

The old guitar won't be sold. The money it
would fetch would never cover the enjoyment that the
odd night of singing brings, and there is no other way to
buy that! A red fifty dollar bill casts a shadow over the
cherished guitar. And singing nights. But, soon enough,
the rheumatic fingers can't play anyway, and it's been a
year, and the instrument gets sold to pay off the money
lenders' fees.

Internet connections are stolen. The opportunity
to steal approaches as a new friend, it becomes one
which is scanned for in many situations, although it
comes unbeckoned. And it leaves unheeded.

Much more often than not, $50 eludes those in poverty.
With decisive and formidable regularity. No one living
in poverty goes anywhere on Saturday night. They don't

go anywhere at all. And if the person living in poverty had a choice between stores, and the surplus cash on hand to allow for the choice to buy in bulk, they would delight in the decision. And if the poor person suddenly, for whatever reason, had a phone and could pay to re-store service, the first thing they would do is call their mother and catch up on the news.

A poor person with a bank account and pre-authorized debits to creditors finds themselves spending 10% of their entire monthly income on Not Sufficient Funds charges levied by the bank. Eventually the bank account has to go – if the bank will release them.

People grow fatigued because they are always making choices about whether to buy eggs or milk; whether to buy cooking oil or bread; always juggling the cupboards against themselves. If there is no flour, there is no need for oil to make bannock. If there is no bread, there is no need for margarine. If there is no sugar, there is no point in buying a box of fruit to preserve. If there is no margarine, there is no point in buying popcorn. If there is no popcorn, there is no point in buying nutritional yeast. It's not in the budget to buy flour, popcorn, oil, butter, nutritional yeast, seasonal fruit and sugar all at once. With what rationale does one choose groceries?

This dilemma is publicly acknowledged by the peoples' government in the following way: at the checkout counters of large grocery stores is a ubiquitous, yet small, sign advising shoppers that families living in poverty regularly have to decide between buying groceries and paying the rent. And would that shopper like to donate $2 to the local food bank? This amount can be added to their bill and the funds delivered to the food bank – very convenient.

Judging by the constant crisis of over-subscription and under-provision, food banks are not receiving $2 from most shoppers. The shoppers might very well think that poverty relief must be a function of the taxes they are already paying. The same shoppers may very well be within one or two lost days of work from needing to visit the food bank themselves. These shoppers do not, however, appear to be concerned with the government's appeal to them personally to make up the shortfall, nor are they petitioning for a raise in taxation or perhaps a redistribution of public spending to address the problem which is being neatly passed off to their good will where it obviously remains unresolved.

Materials provided by the Food Bank are questionable. Some boxes of cereal have worms in them. Worms become kitchen moths and take over every packet of fruit that's been carefully dried in summer abundance. Boxes and cans of preserved items are expired. A single frozen item is always expired, and one wonders at what point was it frozen? But one cherishes the Food Bank. One gives up two hours of work to get what they give, because what they give is worth ten hours of work, rotten or not.

We are talking here about people with an address and a bank account when we talk about people who rely on the food bank. You can't access the food bank without an address and a bank account that shows you have less coming in than going out.

Only a very special few people volunteering in community service organizations seem to realize that human beings require a little more than food. And if they are to become fully realized, or even contributing members of society, they need a lot more. They need stable housing; tech; presentable clothes; work clothes; work!; cleaning and grooming stuff; transportation; education; finance capital; everything that makes the middle classes (we won't speak of the one percent here) able to do the things that make them successful. And until they can generate those purchases on their own, they need a "Tech Bank" and a "Clothes Bank" and a "Bus Pass" bank and a "Work" bank and a "Tool" bank – etcetera. This society is in a significant deficit when it comes to the equipment of the poor.

Poverty fatigue is the gradual, eventual acceptance of the idea that there isn't enough, and the realization that there isn't going to be enough next week, or next month or next year either. It really means "giving in" to the exhaustion. Because giving up is not as hard as trying to imagine that there must be "something better" just around the corner, and the constant disappointment.

It becomes "poverty consciousness" at later stages when the character of an individual is marked by their diminished beliefs and expectations of themselves and their prospects; their personal importance in the scheme of things. Lack of resource begins to seep into one's own manner of thinking, eroding creativity and constructive optimism. "I am poor" becomes a central feature of identity. One is perpetually aware of the cost of things, the want for things. One watches the vision of opportunity drift past, unwilling to test whether it's a mirage. Because it probably is. One also is aware of the need to cloak the wanting grasping habit and the collapsed face, if they are to cling to any connections in the larger world. It is a difficult mantel to manage.

Excuses are needed. "I'm sorry, I can't go out with you – terrible deadline approaching, I have to stay in and try to meet that." Lies are needed. "We just didn't feel up to making the trip." You never go anywhere. When you do go out and walk past shops, your head is pointed deliberately straight ahead at the sidewalk because nothing that is in any of those shops is within your reach. After some years there is no need to deliberately point the eyes ahead – even the idea of going shopping has faded.

Trying to hide the reason why there is no attendance at the birthday party: couldn't afford to bring a present. Trying to justify the failure to show up. Of course, there was no money for the fare, or the expense of participation. A naturally generous spirit becomes hard to recognize when the extent of generosity allowed by the poverty circumstance has been reduced to providing a cheap bottle of wine at an anniversary party. The cost of the sacrifice will never be recognized by the recipient – and in fact they might be insulted. Planning, when all these factors have to be taken into consideration, is a little more complicated than jotting dates on a calendar.

In poverty consciousness, one begins to act and live in the expectation that the rent will not be paid on time. One always has a plan, month to month, for where to go if the landlord is expected of finally losing patience. The plan is never a good one. It can involve fraud, theft, garage sales of all that is held dear, humiliating trips to the pawn brokers for whatever is held too dear. Well before this time the moneylenders, who charge 29%, have all been used and are sending unpayable bills of their own. Prostitution, gambling, and selling drugs on the street, these will be considered once the address is gone.

Perhaps dealing drugs and prostitution are "bad" actions which anyone should feel "guilty" about. But the person who is driven to do those things to get by has long since felt "bad" and "guilty" - that is how poor people feel.

The poor become isolated: unable or unwilling to make a space for themselves, such as they are, in the world as it has been explained to them. They can't see themselves there, in the car commercials and the Disneyland holidays. For some reason, the poor always seem to have a TV in which not to see themselves.

Work, or employment, is a point of heated discussion among the poor who receive social assistance or welfare. If one works full time for $11 per hour, at the cost of transportation and appropriate dress and grooming and lunches away from home and oftentimes babysitters, is it worth it? Is it even possible? Social assistance payments are not enough to relieve any of the problems mentioned so far, and every dime that assisted person earns for themselves is deducted from their support payments, an interesting deterrent to working harder.

When a job does break the surface of the welfare ceiling and offer something more to cling to, it becomes the master of the household. Nothing and nobody is as important as that job. One breaks a finger or a toe and work cannot go on – but work must go on. One does not bother with doctors and radiologists. One cannot miss work, whatever the diagnosis. The broken bone must get better; life must get better. The odd injury will only add to the wealth of tales to be told grandchildren. Crutches are concealed from employers or clients, weaknesses too. One must not appear weak. Rheumatism walks in the front door.

Poverty-stricken parents of children spend too much on cigarettes and beer because the next day is too hard to be faced without some kind of buffer; without some kind of self-inflicted confusion that provides temporary relief from the calculating of dollars and cents against bills. Poverty fatigue exacts relief by intoxication. This is too often the first balance to be adjusted when money comes.

Poverty relief is, firstly, a sedative or depressant. For all the god-abandoned ways of "helping" the poor, the first need is invariably overlooked. These people need anesthetics. Poverty is a pain. That is the unpleasant look on the face of people on the street – pain. This pain can prevent a person from being able to think, to plan, to take stock, to put aside the anesthetic long enough to surmount economic problems. Pain makes it difficult to stay in the moment – even a good moment.

Why do people come to believe their situation is never going to change? Why do they not work night and day and really focus on making money and not spending it, and pick up every bottle and can they see when they're walking, and leave no chance unexploited? Because their situation really isn't going to change, and here's the math. Okay, she's picking up bottles and cans. Is that before or after she gets the kids to school? It's often at night while the children are sleeping. After six months of picking up cans every spare moment, and the unpayable bills have been paid, she has managed to buy the tools she needs to do some service – washing windows – and the clothes and shoes and printed flyers for it too. Now she can pick up cans all night and wash windows in the day time. She is receiving welfare, going to the Food Bank once a month as allowed, using the coupons for the farmer's market, and she has used up her single ticket to access a clothing program. Her children can't have any of the toys or gadgets their school mates have, nor new clothes, ever; and they can't have birthday parties or go to movies or anything with a ticket price.

The window washing is very successful but she

cannot expand because of the liability involved with hiring an assistant. The odds are too powerful and the five different people she has tried, on an occasional cash-at-the-end-of-the-day basis, were hopeless. They almost destroyed her relationship with each client she brought them to. So she is washing windows every day and is now ineligible for welfare, her earnings having gradually cancelled out more and more from her monthly subsidy. And that's what she's doing: washing windows an average 6.5 days a week. Eventually her vehicle will need repairs; her tools and household items will need replacing; she must have to buy something for her kids at some point; it's unlikely that neither she or her two children will ever need to stay home with a cold or flu; and any of a hundred basic inevitabilities will set her back to borrowing money she can't repay and going back under water.

Escape from this situation requires intervention. It's not a Hollywood movie: the single mother, the grad student, the injured foreman – none of them can make it with another student loan or co-op housing or with any amount of work. They have no capital. The best anyone hopes for is a sustainable job that pays the rent and the bills, and the chance to do other work on weekends. People who have to struggle against dreadful odds for their claim to the human condition have often produced compelling words, art, music, and even systems for the society of which they are part. Maybe their own wit and skill was all they ever had. Their triumph in the age-old themes of survival bring meaning and insight, as well as compassion and innovation, to the world they live in; to their neighbours and fellow citizens. They are inventors of systems and arts. But these people, the poor, are less and less a part of a society and more and more they are nameless, numberless desperation which yields up humanity to ignorance and want.

"Compassion fatigue" is what people who witness and try to stem "poverty fatigue" are experiencing. The front line workers are not experiencing poverty fatigue, they are witnessing it: and they grow tired of this, tired of trying to help something that cannot be helped because there are no personal solutions to political problems, and that is compassion fatigue. The political problem in this case is the refusal of those who have enough, who make enough, to give up their assumed identities as superior citizens – and therefore the impoverished people who confirm that assumption.

Poverty is compounding. We know now that one poor generation leads to a next generation of under-educated, under-developed, unworldly people – who marry someone else in the same demographic and reproduce themselves with little exception. At the same time, a more wealthy class of people educates and empowers their youth and those young adults marry each other, prosper, and invest further in their own children. Those children believe they must be inherently superior – an assumption their parents do not contradict in spite of the obviousness of the circumstances they have contrived;

factors which are entirely impersonal.

How does someone dress when they believe themselves to be incurably poor; a statistical burden on their society; a pointless inconvenience to better people? How do they talk? How do they keep their home, or behave, or relate to others?

Powerlessness is compounding. Lack of education and training, lack of development of talents, lack of opportunities – some of which are caused by even the most simple expressions of disadvantage as under-groomed appearances; all this breeds experiences of rejection, disappointment, despair, personal inadequacy. And these experiences totally inhibit development along whatever lines of opportunity may not have been interrupted by economic preference.

All our people should have the right of reply to the central questions of identity that arise in any mind. Am I something this world needs? Do I have something to offer? Can I do something of value, or learn to do it, or even contribute a little piece to something larger than myself; something important? Can I help someone else do something important – something I believe in?

Refusing the poor the opportunity to contribute by assigning a negative value to these people is adding insult to injury. It is also a sort of economic anti-immunity disease. Countless skills and trades could be plied by those who are already on welfare – if only the social workers' salaries and funds could be reassigned to more imaginative and connected, more results-driven programs matching willingness to the extensive and generalized needs manifesting throughout cities and towns and rural areas. Technology, animation and Artificial Intelligence may be replacing jobs but the raw force of the unemployed could be better directed, and trained, valued, used and uplifted in the same stroke. Put some of those resources in the creative hands of The Great Unwashed and the gate-keeping tactics of the rich, masquerading now as social problems, would be transformed.

The gate-keeping tactics are surely conspicuous. A single poor, urban person who lives to be 65 has paid at least half a million dollars, in today's money, into other people's mortgages. For this, they do not even get a credit rating.

The desperation of the poor has given rise to many industries, most notably the new and expanding quick-money lenders. It's an entirely new branch of the financial industry, charging 300% interest. All the outlets have signs on their walls announcing the highest legal rate and that's what they charge. For example: a $300 loan will be repaid at $350 two weeks later.

The poor are worth $2 billion annually to the child apprehension program of the Ministry of Children and Family Development. The children are almost always seized for "neglect," which is not a good description of the real reason – poverty. Then the Ministry subsidizes another household to foster the children, providing more money and services than were ever available to the original family. Hundreds of lawyers need

nurture no other career than taking in the Ministry's re-
ferrals – the parents of the seized children – for Legal
Aid billables. Nothing beyond filing the correct forms
and occasionally showing up in court or at mediations is
required: the lawyers don't have to be successful or even
interested to maintain a steady clientele. The clientele
don't have a choice and it is in the lawyer's financial interests to leave his clients' children in a situation that
causes them to require his services. The largely unquali-
fied psychopaths who, after memorizing a certain line
from the Child Protection Act, can call the police and
bodily remove children with their assistance, seem to do
so without the requirement of just cause. Social workers,
hospital-based social workers, court clerks, and enough
professionals to write a blockbuster soap opera are required – and subsidized by the tax payer – to torment
poor families. But it certainly keeps their position static
and reinforces key beliefs about dignity, equality, charity
– or lack of which.

The poor have largely made the restaurant industry possible. The first major street-front event that happened after rental housing in Vancouver disappeared last
year was that restaurants and cafes started closing all
over. Apparently only one family per restaurant can
make a decent living, while the servers, cooks and dish
washers live hand to mouth, month to month. This same
schedule of remuneration is what makes almost every
service business feasible for the owners, from the oil-
change places to the fashion retailers to the delivery
guys.

Guaranteed minimum income is not a Canadian invention, but there is a trial of this type of subsidy happening now in one of the eastern provinces. One of the main objectives in this socialized financial guarantee is to minimize suffering, among other things.

Recall the time you played Monopoly, and the person who owned most of the board and had all the money then suddenly started lending money to the other players? So they could pay him when they landed on his square? He wanted to keep the game going. In Monopoly, the game ends when one player has acquired so many of the properties, with houses and hotels, that the other players eventually go bankrupt from paying him whenever they land there. In real life, the game ends when one person owns everything and the other players topple the system that made it inevitable that one person, or one percent of people, would own everything – even though that system has been reinforced over generations by a sort of entrained cannibalism among the lower classes. The game ends and a new one begins.

What's in it for someone with a guarantee that they will be able to survive, just barely?

No more $80,000 phrases from academia do we need. How many soup bowls have been filled by the slogan "decision fatigue"? How many rooves raised, feet shod, tools and supplies distributed?

From where do the program resources come, and from where the academic accreditation, for students of the *status quo* to mull and consider and share and discuss and document and research – and finally arrive – at this finely-wrought distinction between "decision fatigue" and "poverty fatigue"? A fund designated the better to understand how the poor feel? To apply a more efficient Band-Aid during psycho-analysis; or explain away the problem of poverty as if it was a personal, not a much wider political and economic, reality?

Well, the poor know how they feel. They are fucking angry. But, unfortunately for evolution, they are also depressed. Worse – they are in denial. Perhaps they are more accurately in a $2.5m psychosis, induced by at least 150 coated-pill-words chanted at them by social workers, food bank volunteers, police, job-seek coaches, etc.

The poor in Canada today have almost certainly spent at least ten years in the public education grade-school system. Was it there where they learned that it was an option to despair? Was it there where they were taught about the statistical reality of poverty?

When you swallow that pill, when you accept that you are inadequate as you are and you require help just to do what others do normally and naturally, then you have broken something harder to heal than a finger or toe.

It's a mistake to go searching after reason for the premise on which the $80,000 Bachelor Degree wordsmiths are trying to "help" the poor – even when their assistance amounts to helping the poor to live in poverty (and denial) more comfortably: emotionally or otherwise. The best explanation for academic interest in naming the experience of the poor, in defining them into a static position, is to make the middle class *themselves* feel better – and to justify taking comfortable, pensionable jobs to "help" society.

Anyone who is not poor, and particularly those who wring their identity from a tear-sodden blanket of castrated-by-privilege compassion, requires a logical, meaningful, and – most importantly – non-intrusive, non-threatening, undisruptive way to name those people whose station makes possible the whole inherently conservative hierarchy of power and place in which the academics and their liberal ilk wish to continue to find themselves comfortable. Under their aegis, the poor can't even own their own poverty when being identified. They have "decision fatigue" instead.

God forbid the poor should be allowed into universities, where they would gore the fatted flank of institutional self-justification with facts, and immediately re-write the analysis of social strata from their own position. They might make the existing deans and professors emeriti obsolete – along with their required textbooks and accompanying royalties from a captive student body.

The poor are now in well-informed, literary, costly and professional denial – much thanks to those who are well paid to define this aspect of their condition. Worse, the poor are convinced.

What should we really wish to hear of the impoverished people? "The poor are revolting!"

Observations on our condition traverse socialist, anarchist, feminist, populist, egalitarian… boxes. Now is the time for each of us to detach our personal identities from those constructs, not shelter smugly, deafly, within them; and to share what is immediately material to our situation and actively take in – or reject – what is being shared by others. The anti-elite are few. The line-ups for barley and circuses (64" TVs) are long. The cost of entertainment is nothing, compared to the value of the work done by those who are hypnotized by the spectacle – and they even re-invest their wages in the hypnotic process. Even the working poor can afford their own hypnosis.

But if they didn't want it, if they have something critical to suggest about how society allots place, our graffiti is illegal – else our poor words, our revolting art, would echo off the city walls. Demanding work: any work! Demanding notice, demanding the chance for a meaningful place. Demanding tools, space, time.

Recent reports in the daily news state that 10% of the British Columbia population owns more than 50% of the wealth in the province. And 50% of the population of BC owns less than 3% of the wealth.

In 2015 Canada was reviewed by the Human Rights Committee, under the provisions of the International Convention on Civil and Political Rights. Many representatives of civil society sent parallel reports to the Committee to highlight areas where Canada is not meeting the human rights standards set out in the Convention. The single most common reference made by these Non-Governmental Organizations and by academics was to poverty. They all wrote about an "alarming" rise in homelessness; the perilous position of the working poor; the sudden increase in people earning incomes that fall below the poverty-line; hunger; a growing trend in worker exploitation consistent with the over-abundance of available workers.

When viewed by the detached and dignified soul, poverty fatigue looks like the snuffing out of candles on the altar. Imagine that someone has lit more candles for more reasons than they can pray for, and they have to snuff some of them out. That's what poverty fatigue is like. Loss. Dreams are extinguished – one cannot afford the mental energy to keep them. The pain of hopelessness in the face of wished-for visions is, scientifically speaking, too biologically expensive to endure. One simply forgets them. It is an act of self-defense even while being an act of self-destruction. But the difference is too subtle to consider when there isn't even enough time for dreams.

These candles, this altar, represent the development of a life. And the candles represent the occasional meanders of life's stream – experience and exchange – which are cut off. In place of an outgoing, well-rounded, contributing person there is a middle-aged, deficient, needy, darkened character with baggage, and tired of packing it.

When some fellow decides to call the media and announce he is going to live on less than $1 a day for the next year, in England, proving that "poverty" is rubbish made up by users, he is not making a fair comparison. Aside from the fact that he is going to live in his own house while he does it, there's an unnoticed, unequal handicap which illuminates a vast blind spot in the perspective of his kind. How can he do it, and not others? Because he doesn't have the problems that poverty has worn into the others. He is educated and he has some discipline – and discipline has worked for him in the past. He doesn't owe favours all round. He doesn't have very dear friends who desperately need his $1 ration that day. He is buoyed up by the knowledge that the austerity is only for a fixed time. And most of all, he believes he can do it.

The question of whether middle class people want to be surrounded by a growing number of the other characters, the ones who do not believe in themselves or much of anything anymore, deserves meaningful consideration. The answering denial and delay of "further study" and experimentation at the moment has possibly not been carefully assessed, nor the impacts anticipated.

History's End (no date)

Just as trans-dimensional childhood memories are rubbed singular and thin by responsible adult doubt, the variegated stories and marvels of a continent's past have been made smooth and impenetrable by the grindstone of this last age. In a post-robotics modern world, where the seas and forests of life have been emptied or reserved behind the weirs and fences of farms owned by someone else, crude aspects of "making do" immunize us, the people, to the complexity of events that brought us here. The sheer volume of disconnected chores and measured, mundane responsibilities weary the hearts and insult the minds to the exclusion of the past, of wonder; and to the excess of opiates. We are not sure why.

We have all grown up without the faintest start as to who our ancestors were – much less why they were who, and even the question itself was only ever vaguely noticeable as inarticulate. Who are we now?

Once upon a more distant time, but not a lost time, the Celts who lived over the lake were fishing off the front porch and laughing at the mice and rats who couldn't reach their stored food. They were laughing because they were rich and happy, they had time for their talents and lived freely, they lived life deliberately. They were the main characters in their own stories. They enjoyed identity and it was directly connected to the world they thrived in. And the world they thrived in relied on them; rewarded them in a spectrum of experience beyond today's seeing.

At that time in history, we owned very little. On the other hand, we owned ourselves: owned our senses and everything they could take in. We owned our place in our little countries, with our long histories and deep pride and wide horizons.

Then the Romans abruptly overran the mice and the rats and the Celts and chopped down those poles which held the cabins, almost magically, above the lake. They overran until they reached the seas and the oceans of Western Europe. The Celts became slaves, or died fighting, or retreated with nothing to places with no one. The Romans told them who they were and fit them into humble passages within the foreign Scriptures of a single almighty God that was carried with them as the thick end of their wedge. The thin end of their wedge consisted of a fine steel blade, and unconscionable thieves - prepared to represent and sell out the free people – were in the middle. Roads were built, all leading back to Imperial Rome. The roads all came from Rome. Crops and trees and minerals were travelled along them, away from the peoples; the plague came back by the road and the peoples grew thin.

Their songs were forbidden. And so were their spiritual ceremonies. And the gatherings of the kings, and the queens' festivals, and the kings and queens themselves. And their spiritual leaders.

The oncoming imperial soldiers had been hardened against centuries of skirmish at the edge of their borders and in stone cities at home, while being subsidized by the military secondment of softer ground inland, and slavery, and they had overthrown their Greek tutor using his own pointed sophistications. (The Greeks had thrown out the Celts before that.) The soldiers belonged to a people whose saviour had his liver eaten out by a vulture every day as punishment for helping them; whose gods killed their own father; whose matriarchs murdered children. Their civilization clung to a rock over the sea, above its noisy and endless argument with the land of the southern Mediterranean shore; witnessed how it rolled one way and crashed against and then rolled back to break again. Those soldiers learned to do the same, but their angry wave kept rolling and breaking on Europe until it reached Scotland. They lived by the sword and their whole nation's humanity moved as one to wield the blade. An entire sea behind a wave.

God's soldiers overthrew the peoples of our lands, annexed our lands – the lands overshadowed to the north and west by the Caucus mountain range. God's servants selected regional kings and princes according to the fervor of their desire for power from the east, where the sun rose beyond the Caucuses and beyond our causes. God's officials decorated newly minted local regents and declared them in the sight of God and God's horses carried them back and forth from Rome, if God's new slaves didn't carry them in sedans. His Holiness, the

Emperor, approved the Pope and then the further representatives on behalf of God and royal blood flowed divine throughout the continent which had previously supplied its own holy blood.

The story of someone else's right was used as the backbone and the hand of every local despot's momentary whim, from today's Russia and Chechnya to Britain and Ireland and Spain. The right to interpret God had endowed those opportunists with a range of rationale to justify their desires – and such a grip they had on evolutionary selection! – since the Roman soldiers had offered convincing, putrifying proof that their God was right. That evidence had been strung up in the streets or hoisted on posts. And since God was from quite far away at the other end of the Mediterranean Sea, so the new rulers of Europe were content to rely on His edgy and self-important go-betweens' discretion to confirm their expedient judgments whenever necessary.

In that Holy Story there were no dragons and no heroes; no warrior queens; no vast constellations of stars as old as time; no language written in plant symbols; no sprawling societies reveling in the spoils of peace; no tribal peoples who were not also heathens to be vanquished.

The peoples of the wolf, the whale, the salmon, the bear, the serpent dragon and the raptor turned against their totems. Eventually. Those bearings in the living land came to mean nothing more than a reminder of pain and grief and loss, everything they represented having been slain or made unrecognizable by torture, or appropriated to a new King's usage. The peoples stitched themselves into the Holy Story, needing the only surviving human fabric, the only story that was permitted by the heirs to the Roman conquest, for anchor. After a time. And the Romans found it convenient to accommodate those patches.

The rivers of story were dammed by the criminalization of languages. The open meadows where family lineages began with a love song were turned to Papal estates. Even the unapproachable snow-capped crags were fenced, cleared, set up with herd animals to feed foreign populations, or blown apart by mines that gouge at veins of metal. Minerals made of time, other times, times now forcibly forgotten – for the invader's fear of their sheer magnetism. The newcomers, the invaders, the colonizers only wanted the metal, and not the transcendence, the ancient ceremonies that improve a base experience to universality.

But the people lived. They raked charred fragments from the hot ashes of their countries and found themselves recognizable. They sang according to the lullabyes they remembered, they danced according to the muscles they used most in their region's work. The conqueror's rationale, and his elaborate Story, remained the bit in the bloody mouths of their new kingdoms. The peoples assembled reflections of themselves with threads of their local stories that had withstood the borrowing and the trimming of the Holy Story of Rome; the Story retreating Celts had saved in Ireland – the prize of civilization! Now their sacred festivals were called Easter; Christmas; Hallowe'en; still those belonged to them and they remembered. The solstice of the summer, however, was sacrificed to the height of extortionist agricultural labours.

The new royal kings set about expanding their divine powers and ransomed men's families to charge their sons, armour clad, south and east, to drive away the partners of the past, the now "infidel" Moors, the Arabs and Asians: to seize their trade.

This God had turned his back on Asia, closed his doors to Persia, locked his bridges to Africa, and kept the keys under cover of the Story of Divinity and Right-eousness, in the sanctuary of Dominion and Discovery, in the Vatican.

For many generations the genius and heart of Europe was condemned to amnesia, isolation and taxation. Their own economies and all the tools, technologies, thoughts, boats and freedoms that made it flow: these were not required to serve Rome. The profits of organized back-breaking labour accumulated and were distilled by highly privileged trade in silk, spice, medicine, gold and perfume, in Rome.

After endless centuries, the benefit of this Imperial Empire disappeared from Europe and even Britain, along with the soldiers. But the rationale remained.

Now a thousand years of warring over delegated royal powers had scarred divisions along the old trails of market, and borders kept people in and kept people out.

The palaces of Paris, London, Versailles, Naples, Brussels and Madrid bloomed endlessly more exquisite under the regional overlords. Control of the lands once animated by tribal peoples became tractable, and the places became known as France, Austria, Belgium, Switzerland, Germany, Italy, Armenia, Spain and England.

The kings' families grew. They fought and starved and married each other to maintain their perch atop a society yoked by betrayal and greed and deception. The poor people gave their sons to the armies on pain of death, and they got death, one way or the other. They got it early.

Once everything had been taken away from the people, the Kings occasionally consented to permit certain actions and protections. The people had long since forgotten what licenses once belonged to men and women naturally, through ceremony, or by deed, of their own jurisdictions, in their own lands. Now Royal Declarations, Proclamations and Decrees described the usages of limited rights which men and sometimes women could exercise by the grace of the King, and this bought the kings some time. But plagues bred in the slums of people who could not travel or had nowhere to go and nothing to do. The "witchcraft" of herbal medicine had been burned out. The old sciences were completely lost to the peoples now shackled to fields, now nothing more than a certain type of animal crop which harvested another type of vegetable crop.

Industry grew exponentially in the encampments

built to contain talented villagers who would pay tribute to the Kings' men for the freedom to work with their minds. But their fingers were being worked apart by splintering tools. The necessity to increase production at last persuaded God to make his geographic philological walls permeable to technologies of industrial merit. The inventors and engineers travelled to India and China and Africa again. They drove themselves harder and the bonds to their tasks kept them focused on tighter loops, better leverage, more efficient curves, new materials: industry bred industry. Mechanization came of the union between economic necessity and mercy for the people's splitting fingertips. The Kings always wanted more.

Workers specialized in different parts of different machines. The specialists left the village and new cities absorbed them. The talented young people had to leave to follow the specialists, and rarely did they come back. The cultures bled youth into the pumps and pistons of an incalculable machine that had eaten their homelands and coughed out palaces and slums many miles away.

The ones who sought supplies for these expanding industries went farther in boats that had been redesigned and equipped with navigational instruments found back and beyond the Pope's onetime velvet geopolitical curtain.

And the good Book was its own sentinel, amplified by artists who worked for the church – the best paying client since it had all the taxes on every economic exchange. The best artists were cultivated. The pounding hearts and hammers of the sculptors exalted a Creation attributed to the good Book of their benefactor, so the people thought Creation came from the good Book.

The seafaring interpreters and agents of God's imperial decree marshalled islands, elaborate strings of islands and whole continents to the largely metallic glory of the few, those Holy few, who would fulfill ever greater meanings of Dominion which had been set down in the elite script of the priests. Boats full of ore, timber and fish returned to the little continent – west of the Caucasus: in barges along the Rhine, the Rhone, the Thames and the Liffey. The big boats set forth again with men as the ballast. Men and pigs, boys, sheep, cows and horses. The Holy few did not need so many peasants at home; they needed to disperse them and their herds around the globe – once they admitted it was a globe. The Kings' captains raced out on a gentlemen's agreement that wherever no Christian prince was discovered, the first to arrive with a cross could claim the place.

And so they did. The poor, beaten peasants who sailed for new lands had no recollection of freedom and when they arrived on foreign shores they slaughtered anyone they encountered who possessed it; anyone who could not show shackles on their hearts and minds. They traveled the world, they began to empty it, they did to others what had been done to them. After more than one thousand years the peoples who had lost their lands, their names and identities were rewarded with privilege, position and power akin to that which the vengeful, the opportunist and the despicable had seized from them under the armoured gaze of Roman conquerors.

Trade in annexation, looting and colonization eventually allowed the merchants to win out over the kings, but they, like the kings, allowed the Book to live on. It was effective. And so they kept the kings as well. The kings had been made by the Book. The church maintained a friendly arrangement with the states, blessing their monarchies and sitting on the side of the business hand, the land-holding and administrative side.

Seventy-eight thousand years of evolution, of blossoming, of observation, of recording, of piling rocks and re-piling them just so, of war and fire and flood and faith had fallen in. And perhaps it was not for the first time that history's tale was abbreviated by an attempt on the future. It was no one's fault. No one in particular – just the people who were waging the land race and running the human war.

Two thousand years later, now, the stone passage tombs at Newgrange and Louth and Douth have since been dug out of time's own covetous soil army – those star worshipping crypts older than the pyramids and still watertight. The cave paintings of brother bison were lit again; the islands' names: Jersey, Guernsey, still hold their own truth of legendary cows emerging from the sea when the people needed milk – and yet graciously continue to nod under the more recent iron bells of Saint Peter and Saint Helier. The Celt's poles and cabins and rafts have been excavated from under parking lots in that part of Switzerland which is now Zurich. No one re-members what it all means, except that there used to be a different way. The distant past does not speak. Not in its own voice.

Now when the church bells at the business bank-ing end of Lake Zurich deafen the birds on a Saturday night, their clanging creates enough friction on the air to cauterize the week's thoughts. The bells of the many churches at once fire the streets with such a panic and resounding urgency, reverberating through the stone am-plifiers of towers, vibrating the body temple, unseating the fragile immortal soul, deafening the everything spirit; and the mind races and the clothes must be starched and the clock must be set and there is tomorrow to think of and whether the children will properly recall the mass – cuff them again! This is serious. The same bells ring out around and around the world and the fume of powerlessness is inhaled… *God grant me the serenity to accept that which I cannot change.*

There had been something beyond this being summoned and being released by the bells of the Book keepers at one time.

One legendary argument for an older way is that when the Romans had come to the lake at Zurich and cut off the three Celtic heroes' heads, that trio of pagan and savage refusers reached down and picked them up. The headless leaders made their way back atop the hill from which they had descended to confront the new god's missionaries, and when they got to the top they put down their heads, doubtless with a view over the lake, and gave in to the body's vulnerability to decapitation.

There had been something else to that story, perhaps even more to one of the stories that one of those men might have told one of their children on some exceptional occasion. A church stands today on their buried, wordless skulls.

Our story, the peoples' stories, have been appropriated by the powerful, and we written out of it. That country we call History was invaded and looted of all our inheritance, even the knowledge or our birthright. It seems now, by these history books, as if only Holy Roman kings and queens have ever acted in Europe, and before their coming there was only chaos. As if stone observatories and silver necklaces and passage tombs arose retroactively to satisfy royal amusement, without builders or engineers; or accidentally. As if knowledge of the stars and the solstices and the elements was mischance, without science; animal scratch.

Our day-to-day coming and going in this age is as regimented as the legions which spread, a humanity-consuming plague, across the white tribes of Europe.

There was a time when we, ourselves, were "the book." When it was our very selves woven into sections on the loom of history, in the colours of our houses, in the fibres of our lands. When we were the fingers of action raveling story to life and life to story; when we stood up and the cloth of pages trailed behind us as we went; when we were life itself and decided its meaning.

Now we move like dusty leaves fallen from the dead end of a book written somewhere else, by someone else, thousands years ago.

WOMEN'S DAY

The first time I went to a women's day celebration, I felt like an imposter. I felt sore like a stuck out thumb; like my disguise was inadequate; so that I was forced to ask myself: who was I spying for?

"I have a hard time relating to women because they are always acting like doormats or play things," I said in the closing circle. They. Being a woman never seemed like a smart thing to own up to in this world. The weaker sex, the butt of jokes, the one whose needs never matter.

I cast around for some positive identification with my femininity. Did I have femininity? Maybe in the hereditary sense, I think my grandmother had it. But me, possibly not since I saw it used against my mother, or since I was ridiculed for wearing a pink plastic hair clasp at about the age of eleven - "ah, look: Kerry's wearing a barrette!" Guffaws from my male class mates. I only had male classmates as a child, in a one-room school house out in the sticks. No pun.

Not that I had never experienced a female power that could freeze the balls off a brass monkey. I like that metaphor because of course it's the sea that would have frozen those particular cryptic balls off the cannon ship - the sea, the ultimate she; her I could get with. But not the woman that calls the image to mind - my primary schoolteacher, whose bosom was such an overpowering thing it had the effect of an ill concealed and deadly weapon. Early sexual memories are assuredly scarred by the negative influence of those orbs of Gaia on my school fellows. They were terrified of them, jutting into their faces when they did something wrong.

The feminine - the only part of the species that could be fat. Women, whose sexuality was either explicitly denied by ranching hard survival, or was in itself a raison d'etre - albeit one that was considered poor. Women are the only ones who can do something wrong sexually.

Standing in a circle of what were undoubtedly women, I wondered, is this a support group? We were supposed to be talking about our grandmothers. These people had a mixed air. It was like, there was guilt there, like we all knew we were doing something ridiculous. Or maybe it was just mine, one's perceptions are always coloured by one's perceptions. The circle was also mysteriously happy. I wasn't sure if this was sensible. More like being a woman is a cause for much heaving of sighs, resigned sarcasm or out and out mourning. I was embarrassed of the infant girl knocking around inside for a soft spot to peer out at the proceedings. There really wasn't one.

Empowerment means being tough and unyielding, I thought. Success depends on masculine assertiveness and equal rights for all who are not pathetic.

Yes, yes, we've all had babies and isn't that just the most quaint of biological marvels. Yes, sure, the species wouldn't have got far without ovaries in the mix. A faint warming for the memory of my newborn daughter, breastfeeding, those days of pregnancy when it dawned on me that everyone I was looking at had a mother who felt that way for them, at least at some time. Those memories, however, are strangled off by the fact that the male part of that pregnancy had later beat me up, kicked me out of the house with the baby in my arms, literally chased me away and was physically stronger than me. Again, how does being a woman help?

Being a mother is many wonderful things, but not so much when you're on your own. Society will tell you that. You're not much without a man, it says. How are you going to raise that child? How indeed. Pay another woman to look after it while I go out and work shoveling shit in the barn to nearly pay the bills, that's how. Graduate to a job position alongside that woman looking after other children whose better-paid mothers are shoveling other shits of the post-industrial variety.

What right, I demand of no one, do we have to be here celebrating this dependence? Maybe we could all just cry about it. Maybe the only women who should be here celebrating are the ones that look like Pamela Anderson. Maybe they have had a good time being a woman. Have they? I shudder at the thought, which I think with my very rational and quick brains, of being valued for my looks and denied any other redeeming features - a mouth, for instance, and a decent dialectical vocabulary to use it with.

Yes, it is better to sling the tits back tight and act like women were an afterthought. A necessary one, but a doomed one. Let's get on with the accepted game - making progress and pushing back oppression to make a safer space for the weak ones like cripples and mentally retarded people and women. So we can have a revolutionary egalitarian society. Do all these proudly weak women help with that

Speaking of weakness, still standing in the circle, I'm having some. Confusion, maybe. Frustration.

I didn't come here to get all mushy and sing Koombaya, or Womb-baya, or whatever other alternatives My Lord we have come up with to get us through. What about the women who made bullets during the First World War and got us the vote? What about how we get to play ice hockey now? I know I liked it. And if we are celebrating our advancements, which have to do with being able to do what men do, then isn't it absurd to be celebrating *women*? Isn't that just what we don't want to be?

I didn't really want to burst anyone's bubble, they seemed quite happy. And that was puzzling. Clearly there was something about Women's Day that they were experiencing and that I was not. You know how Mr. Grinch has that epiphany that maybe Christmas means a little bit more?

I picture the boxes and bows, the tinsel and trapping that adorn most womanly women - the shawls, the jewelry, the dress. Is there something more to it than a parcel for the opposite sex to unwrap? Men don't dress to be unwrapped, they just are. I certainly don't dress to be unwrapped and will quickly sort out any guy who fails to notice that.

Maybe it's just me who think women dress that way to get unwrapped. Then again, maybe these women have had better experiences after the unwrapping than I have. I try to find the garb attractive; the knee-high red faux leather boots; the dingly earrings; the large and colourful objects hanging from the necks. I'm not sure that my post-industrial culture condones such joyful expressions. Does it? Is it right to adorn? What does Orwell think of it? Wouldn't those things get in the way of work? I think of the grandmother I never met, who died from ovarian cancer after years of rubbing a topical contraceptive around her lower belly.

I thought we were here because we are happy to have equal rights - to be able to wear jeans and steel toed boots. I thought we were here because now we can throw a man in the lock-up if he hurts us, even if we're married to him. I thought women's lib was about voting, owning businesses and getting a fair share of the money after divorce.

I have very few memories of my one surviving grandmother, which began to show up. She was strikingly attractive, always wonderfully dressed. She had poise and dignity, in spite of great difficulties which I learned of later. She was something else, a different generation perhaps, and she watched her waistline and looked good in her impeccably chosen dress suits and dresses. She wore pearls and gold, her hair was always nice and her make-up beautiful and she was always kind. She died when I turned seven. No one took her place.

It was like a door closed, then. My beautiful grandmother died and no one where I lived looked or acted anything like her. When I think about her, I can feel the place where beauty and women lived together, and I can see how far away it is from me. After all that bullet making and power politics, we have maybe become less than what we are. We have grown dependent on our co-opted manliness for our power and our rights. We have let that grandmother really die, really leave - maybe out of pain or grief, maybe out of weakness, not being able to be women and safe in the world. We let her go in place of "advancement" in the work place.

As the tears roll, I feel grateful to her for being who she was. Because she is part of me, she has given me something I still have no matter the smell of the ice rink locker. I think as a child I felt betrayed by her mortality. The fact that she stood out as a woman, and then she died, might have influenced my belief that to be male was to survive. There must be something in me that is capable of respecting the woman I am. The fact of her means there might be something more than the boot-wearing, swearing and defiant bullet making happens-to-be-female woman I am.

Luckily the other women continue to hold international women's day celebrations, for people like me. I get to cry about my grandmother and my boots, once a year.

Since those gatherings, since letting them affect me, I seem to be capable of wearing necklaces that feature things more colorful than buffalo skulls or vertebrae now. I can see attractive women without labeling them. I have discovered that a lot of the way I am, yes, even sensitive, comes from a goddess. There are goddesses, and we are among them. We have the ability to honour them in the way we are.

I realize that I have a different, a better, way of being myself because of Women's Day. It's a gathering of women from very different walks of life who get together because on all those paths we have experienced being discredited for being female. We have had trouble being ourselves because of outdated beliefs like mine, put on us by the beliefs of men and their dominance in our society. We have been marvelously defiant and tough and powerful, and we have done it as women, as goddesses, as the weaker sex, raising babies and nurturing while we fight. We have the right to be vulnerable, and still not be taken advantage of. We have the right to work and receive the benefits of it, and it doesn't have to be work that fuels a war. We have the right to oppose war, and especially so because it is our sons and daughters who are sacrificed. We also have the right to be beautiful - because we are.

The rights of women do not stem solely from the fact that we produce male babies. We are here in our own right, and we have some very powerful things to contribute to the human condition, and some very fragile things.

And I hope that my grandsons some time in the future are not in a position where they feel the only way to express their worthiness and equality, their sensitivity and compassion, is to wear dresses and lipstick. I think now that women do not have to wear boots or cut their hair short to be powerful and influential.

THE POWER
HAS TOO MUCH MEDIA

"Media" is the plural form of the Latin word "medium," meaning in its relevant usage, "an intervening substance, as air, through which a force acts or an effect is produced." We recently came to refer to the newspapers by this definition, and called them *the news media.* We recognized that those materials and the content they carry are indeed a substance through which forces act. Social, political and economic forces. Later radio and television, magazines, the internet, facebook, Hollywood: *media.*

We began to say that *the media has too much power,* meaning that we came to rely more on information carried by those intervening substances, information produced by others, far away, with real interests in forming our opinions on the things that affect our lives and our worlds, than we did on each other or our own experience. We discovered that elections, national attitudes toward relevant issues, child raising and all things could be influenced by the media. Increasingly there are more types of media, more vehicles for media, and more and more global subscribers to these media.

Today there is no question of media having too much power, but the startling reality of *the power having too much media.* For every subtle consumer preference, for every sensitively guarded avenue of human thought, there is a form of media which lulls it and enters and allows power to act through its presence, to be noisily or graphically represented. All manner of media has evolved to reach through every demographic and get right in people's faces; in their ears and eyes and through to their hearts and minds.

Advertisers with products to sell are very interested in reaching these semi-conscious places. They pay well to be carried in by whatever form of media reaches the desired destination in the overall human anatomy.

This has the combined effect of turning us, the subscribers to media, into a product: the consumer of the manufactures on view in the ads that media sponsors itself with. The media competes *for us*, to show the purchaser of the ad content that they have a large and diverse product to offer – a large circulation among potential consumers. The media will do anything to achieve *us*: lie, strip, twerk, stir violence. Perhaps we feel special. So today, *powerful forces act through ubiquitous, scintillating forms of media and we are no longer one of the deciding forces but the object of their actions.*

There is no question that the many forms of media which reach most people, the mass media which the masses access for news of the world, is backed by power. And today, most media is not bringing news of the world. It is bringing a way to deny the world and live as individuals in a personal world, nonexistant, isolated and powerless.

Power has Hollywood: product placement in blockbuster movies is prime real estate, and that placement is one of the diminishing sources of revenue a producer has in the age of digital piracy – so they want to make movies that advertisers agree to on a philosophical level.

Minutes after the Declaration on the Rights of Indigenous Peoples was adopted in UN General Assembly, a movie called "Peeples" opened. It was condescending in its representations of what were clearly land-based, spiritual people who would be labelled "aboriginal" in Canada, or "indigenous" in worldwide legal places. The power has Dances With Wolves, Legends of the Fall, The Lone Ranger. Looking a little more closely, the power has the celebrities who produced those movies. On a more sinister and global scale, it has The Devil's Double, spy movies, "documentaries." It has Downton Abbey, glorifying a completely white cast and purring for a "simpler time," when poor people knew their place and elegance was undiminished by their presence. It has Django Unchained, where the black man's only tool is violent vengeance. It has pop music, where the height of aspiration is one night with a beautiful girl, and white Disney teenagers spank mature black women in live performances broadcast around the world. The power has the History Channel.

But the power has much more media than that. It has ads on all the alternative online news sites, which rely on ads for revenue to keep operating. It has quite alternative websites of its own – googling Malcolm X or Martin Luther King Jr. could land you on a page designed to obscure those historical personalities.

The power actually has whole environmental organizations and their campaign communications – even manufacturing their own opposition within 'watchdog' social sectors and preparing the messages the media will report! The Pew Family Trust is an excellent example, forming the supposed activist group Bear Watch and their well-planned capitulation at the formation of the Great Bear Rainforest Park on the west coast; and Suncor has the Canadian Boreal Initiative and, through it, the Women Advocating Responsible Mining. The irresponsible oil and gas producers founded WARM.

The power has most of the inhabitants of ivory towers, where its intellectual opposition is also carefully cultivated and contained, and the academics "publish or perish."

The power has bloggers to sit on facebook, youtube, news site comment lists and torque the stream of "free public discussion" and expression that happens there. Most people acting individually are not bent on bending that stream, but are easily ready to go along with it. Most individuals seek out available opinions – and they get pre-fabricated imposed ones posing as fellow citizens.

These mediums come to define the words we use to name our worlds.

When babies are learning to speak they can hear all kinds of languages and produce the sounds. As the young people age, by about seven, they become able only to hear the sounds they have heard most and grow less able to hear other sounds – as in other languages. The brain stops keeping those channels open as they seem not to be needed, Like language, the icons and syllables and phrases of the mass, incessant media hydra have become the means of communication of choice available to new First World western generations: it's what they have heard most. The young people of today talk about relationships, "like in The Notebook!" and environmental issues, "like in Avatar!" and heroes, "like in…" – but no longer have a visceral connection to the physical, sensual, emotional, inter-personal world and its creatures portrayed in those movies, nor even words for their names and aspects.

Even those popular forms of media which came out of humble beginnings and reached hundreds of millions through a free internet loophole now suffer *the power* to act through their venue, or actively join it. For instance, when Cop Watch of New York City reached over a million viewers with their video of an instance of police brutality towards a civillian, they received an automatic response from youtube inviting them to participate in an advertising program. But when "youtube" discovered the nature of the organization which posted the video, the offer for cash remittance for advertising was retracted. In an instance from the other end of the spectrum: the owner of facebook met with secret service agents of the USA and of Britain to discuss terms of sharing facebook users' information with the governments, as an anti-terror mechanism. Facebook has made one man a billionaire.

When Marshall McLuhan said *the medium is the message*, he was looking at people sitting still and absorbing widely circulated information without raising much response. He was looking at unilateral platforms like newspapers that may not publish responses to their material if it didn't suit them, to town hall discussions and public art galleries where artists come and engage with people who are seeking, to the theatre of the oppressed, to national radio broadcasting corporations which wear a badge and tell people, without qualification, what's going on, and wondering aloud whether it isn't the actions that a medium provokes that is the real story. He was looking at stories of genocide running down short columns next to large display ads for suburban utility vehicles. He was noticing that there's no place for the world news to land in a person's workday.

The most important simple single fact that supports the idea that the power has too much media in this part of the world is that 99% of print, radio and television media with mass distribution in Canada is corporately owned – and has been for many decades. These media are further corporately backed through advertising - advertisers will want to be pleased with the content which appears alongside their promotions. Corporations buy ads in the media from other corporations, and they control the content of that media because their financial contributions are the most relevant to the owners of the particular media in question.

The power has politicians, elections and governments: its foot soldiers, middle men and buffering bureaucracy of investigation and legislation. Consider that politicians are backed by owners of the same corporations which largely control, or at least contain, the media by their influence.

Whether a local Trustee or a potential Mayor or a runner for an MLA spot, the public candidate's first pledge of allegiance is to a private campaign sponsor. The elected official then rises further by way of the official's discretion in spending currency in contracting for public works, licensing resource industries, and permitting development. They arrive finally to a seat on the Board: deciding who will get the next campaign funding to run for and keep office and perhaps receiving a knighthood. In the same way, former BC Premier Sir Gordon Campbell originally accepted real estate tycoon Jack Poole as his sponsor to run for Mayor of Vancouver, and, in the course of his career, handed over vast tracts of unceded indigenous land near Whistler, paid Poole's companies to build condos on it and then bought them back all with public money. He sold the public railway to his friends, divided the public utility, and spent billions of tax dollars financing transportation infrastructure which hydro-electric producers, oil companies, forestry companies and mines will use to access resources. Resources which are well understood to be situate on unceded indigenous homelands.

Political candidates who don't advocate the power's agenda don't get much media coverage. Their real job is to sell that agenda to the public.

Embedded journalists simply smooth the way for their bosses' candidates and make potential public outcry toothless for want of relevant question. The journalists recognize their ultimate employer – even while obscuring the identity of that agent by minimizing or blacking out recognizable features in their reporting.

For example, in news reports of indigenous protest there is only the question of what should be done with these "terrorists" – not documentation of the atrocious human rights abuses they are resisting and exploration of human rights based legal remedies. Editors place royal weddings in front of world news, as they did while Canadian pilots led the NATO attack on Qaddafi in Libya. The British Broadcasting Corporation, the BBC, agreed at some point with Canada and others that Palestinian killings of Jewish leaders should be called "assassinations" in the press, while Jewish murders of Palestinians would be called "executions." Here at home, in reports of the sale of BC Rail, a public asset that was making money and linking communities, somehow the journalists just cannot find any business or personal connections between the government members and the buyer – they have to rely on what one or two non-conformist politicians believe may have happened and simply quote them.

If the odd elected politician gets batted into the stratosphere on the blunt end of a failed initiative, there are plenty more where he came from, and some will be sacrificed in scandals this way. But that is what it is when the mass media goes after a politician: a failed initiative. He falls in the balance of convenience; a sacrificial lamb to oil the gears of appearance, to appease the gods of The One Truth who must remain concealed. For example, when BC Premier Glen Clark was thrown out on the basis of his, not unusual, use of BC Lottery monies, that had more to do with silencing his growing personal interest in an Inquiry into the events of the Gustafsen Lake siege which was a provincial and federal attempt to wipe out indigenous sovereigntists in 1995. Glen Clark had recently presided over the Nisga'a Final Agreement – no small accomplishment, getting the roadblocking Nisga'a to coerce and intimidate their citizens to vote "yes" to a "treaty" that would make them a BC municipality – but in spite of this victory he could not be suffered his questions. And all BC Premiers have had their hands in the till.

The power's media is held up by essential pillars. For instance, "progress" is above criticism, where progress is an ever-expanding economy making more and more people cash-rich (or making some people more and more cash-rich). It insists on a lack of alternatives. For example, when Tsilhqot'in people blockade their Fish Lake against open pit gold mining, the only debate in the media is how long their sentences should be, and politicians like Rich Coleman pronounce on the gravitas of "turning back the clock" to a fictitious time when Indigenous babies and mothers died in childbirth, lacking the "progress" which gold mines and all that flow from them provide.

In Canada and now in further circles, particularly other British colonies, an essential pillar for media's made-up world, the one in which advertisers wish us to believe we live, is that Canada is an excellent nation. The whole idea of *nations* has been swallowed and digested and excreted and composted to give growth to a modern definition: that a *state* which has imperially gated in the tribal nations on their homelands and made all other individuals equal within its borders, although without any meaningful identity, is a nation. So for instance, while Canada is perhaps an excellent *organization*, the uniting force of indiscriminate resource extraction and structural development on a couple generations of immigrants from desperate situations around the world can hardly be understood as the genesis of a nationality or a people. It's more like an enterprising refugee camp. The fact that the cornerstone of this excellent organization is the dispossession and decimation of a hundred distinct indigenous nations is conspicuous. More to the point, the Canadian dollar has just been made a reserve currency. It must be a safe state for money and the power.

A certain perpetual cataract on power media's discourse vanishes the monopoly that unceded aboriginal title to the land holds on this incorporated state of Canada. And in the shadow and skew of that blind spot, in the denial of a great human crisis, what else is sacred? Can the product of the mass media point out one sacred thing which they have not already discarded along with indigenous peoples? Are children sacred, or communities, or identity?

As the corporations do away with the last undergarments of Mother Nature - they're digging deep now - it is as unlikely a time as any in colonial history for the power media to accurately reflect the legal status of the lands and the question of the survival of the peoples who still own it outright, or else have the right to live on it and have a future on it according to their own determinations.

Entire nations, entire languages, entire histories and cultures are lifted off the surface of the planet by the industrial strength cleansers of humanity present in the cynicism of the media's human products. The same advertisers bringing us the media are the ones whose goods and wares come from the indigenous territories.

In this "news" environment, journalists or reporters cannot simply reach out through a loyal subscription list to people who are hungry for their cutting analysis or up-to-date fact finding; they are simply embedded in the corporate agenda and they work for the power - if they want to keep their jobs. Newspapers in every community in British Columbia are owned by one of two conglomerates – Black or Glacier. Sometimes there are two newspapers in a community, like in Whistler: one belonging to each corporation.

But the sheer *volume* of this type of media creates the appearance of balance or range. Canadians have had a kind of access to information that few else in the world have had. *We have had reporters in every part of the globe for decades*. And we have had cheap TV. This makes Canadians feel informed. But we know what a few artists can do with some celluloid and free reign on presenting the situation in the way that suits the power. The general state of Canadian opinion on world matters is not so much *informed* as it is *manufactured*. What the Canadian army, Canadian mining companies and Canadian international aid funding do next is, well, decided by the power. That power informs the media.

If it were another way, we might not accept the general lie that "the colonial period" in Canada is over: because taking indigenous children from their mothers with police is not a post-colonial act and it happens every day. Incarcerating people who block roads into their lands is not a post-colonial act and that happens at least once a month in Canada. But Canada is valuable to the power, and the media occludes such realities.

If it were another way, we would be made to notice that once the indigenous nations are mostly gone, if they ever succumb to Canadians' genocidal attempts, there are few who will help us when progress comes for us and the places we live, breathe and drink water. For instance, Canadians should come to grips with the fact their governments have already sold the place: the oil and minerals still underground are already paid for; a down payment has been made for the water; multi-national corporate investment in agricultural land and potential hydroelectric power soar. Selective government controls and subsidies drive down the price of land, water, forests: the denial of aboriginal title and criminalization of aboriginal protesters is a government subsidy.

Media produced by human beings and not by corporations might not run ads for an organization called "Reconciliation Canada," which is a company that is valued by the power for creating the appearance that it has something to do with remedying the crimes of Indian Residential Schools. In practice, it just accepts corporate sponsorship to conduct more fund raising for the company, for purposes undeclared. The occasional volunteer-led walk or event happens under their banner. A humanist media might investigate such a company with interest. No justice for one means no justice for *any*one – and falsifying affairs to appear as justice is a shame.

If we had power, we the people, and media that power can afford, we would be forced to reflect and find ourselves immediately and in no uncertain terms guilty of doing nothing when "they" came for the Indians; when the army, the police, the churches and the child-seizing welfare bureaucracy came for the Indians and removed them from the path of "national" "progress." But the "they" is actually "we." So, "we did nothing when we came for the Indians," except that doesn't make sense. We did do something: we came for the Indians. If there was anywhere in the imperially ransacked world where journalism was independent of the power, this might be a readily accepted report.

Some Canadians are calling for First Nations to maintain some control of land, particularly around Independent Power Projects and logging, but it is only out of self-interest, and the "control" is delegated. The legal issues have not just gone away and we know, vaguely, that aboriginal consent is required in certain places in order for industry to plough ahead. We do not, however, as a society, seem to appreciate that none of us last without oxygen, water and wild plants - the memory holders for our cultivated crops.

We must hold our own memory together. We must not foray further into the dangerous wilderness of an individualized myth of personal freedom within a wonderful but strictly static world.

So long as we publish flyers on pulp from the boreal forest, or upload images using molybdenum-enabled hardware, or sit at home and analyze the state of the world privately and in isolation, turning subjects into objects, or accomplish any of the aforesaid with electricity from salmon-destroying dams, we are not seeing the cloud in this computer screen. And if we can't see that, if we are speaking only for our imaginary, disconnected profile-projections without seeing the river in this ink, we are not speaking to our true nature. We are endangering it.

We don't really want entertainment, we really want the truth about ourselves, in all its musical, dramatic and vividly terrible beauty. We just don't know that because we haven't had it; but with those truths, we could act. We don't really want welfare and "social safety," what we really want is power in our own lives and worlds. We want education not indoctrination, and we want enlightenment. We want Medicare, but we want healers and a healthy environment too. We don't just want subsidized housing and child care, we want freedom and fair wages.

When we can't have the truth, we watch cats playing

piano on youtube – after an ad for a car. Probably after coming home from work to pay for that car we need to get to work.

But I don't want to listen to your music on the radio, I want to sing with you. I don't want to read your blog, I want to hear your voice. I don't want to watch you on livestream, I want you here with me. I don't want to watch your cooking show, I want you in my kitchen and I don't want to watch an ad for shampoo while the onions are caramelizing I want to hear again the story about how you got those mangoes when you were in Panama.

COLONIAL FUTURES:
THE DEVIL YOU DO

> *In connection with the land question, and all other matters considered at the Conference, the Committee thinks it important to point out that, while the Indians of this Province are subjects of His Majesty, and an obligation for their protection has been placed upon and accepted by Canada, they are neither wards of the Government nor citizens of the Dominion, and that to this day there is no real relation between the Indian tribe and the people of Canada, the tribe remaining a community not yet part of the Canadian people.*
>
> - British Columbia Indian Conference, Held at Vancouver, 20th to 23rd June, 1916, STATEMENT Issued by the Committee appointed by the Conference, 28th June, 1916

Canadians are people and families who have come here from every place on the earth. They still speak the different languages from whence they came; they dress, eat, act, socialize, invest, study, develop and worship according to widely varying religious and spiritual beliefs. But wherever people came from over the last 300 years, wherever they live now – all across this half continent, whatever they do, and whether they pray in church, mosque, temple, open field or roomy basement, they do so because the English god (and therefore the English king) is better than the gods of the original nations of these lands (and therefore their sovereigns), and that is the basis of the right to live freely in Canada.

It is the Christian God's priority over the gods of these places, here where Canada's map is, which guarantees all "rights" and "freedoms" and "equality" that individuals and families and groups presently expect as Canadians or as guests in Canada.

Oh yes! Didn't they tell you? Check any Supreme Court of Canada ruling: when Great Britain successfully landed a tub on the shore, and someone in it (whoever he was) was capable of lashing together two sticks to make a cross and stood it up on the beach, and proclaimed the King's supremacy; that was it. All the lands in every direction suddenly came under the sovereign jurisdiction of the British King – who was appointed by God.

This is the "legal" foundation of Canada today.

Originally an imperial outpost designed as a resource-extraction warehouse, fenced off against other European colonizers, and populated accordingly, the Canadians have since staged their own sort of War of Independence in the creation of what is basically an enterprising refugee colony. The action of Independence from the British crown was bloodless in itself, even agreed upon, but the Canadians have successfully incorporated their origin story into their own Constitution and the British let them go.

It helps to recall how recently this was. Japanese people who were living here in 1940, and were interned and exhaustively robbed by Canada during the Second World War, later filled out documents for their return to Japan which had them sign off the on the renunciation of their stats as a "British Subject in the Dominion of Canada." Volunteers collecting new voters door-to-door in Vancouver in the 1950s and 60s proffered forms which also required confirmation of the British citizenship of the new registrant.

The symbolic connection to the legitimizing legend of the Holy Explorers is upheld by a picture of the ruling British monarch on every piece of currency, in every school and in every court room and house of governance.

Canadians spent the 20th century worrying that they are not unique, or don't have a common identity, but of course they are and they do. It is not a positive designation. It only means "one who left their own home and economy to build a new home and economy on another's home and at the expense of another's economy."

The state is a Parliamentary, democratic, enterprising refugee colony with its shallow roots tapping every kind of extractive industry, and it remains financially dependent on immigration because economic growth is publicly subsidized and privately gained. Canadians have no historical nor visible cultural or spiritual unification, nor identification with the lands they

drain; no common language or culture, and only act together as a perpetual plantation and resource extraction
camp – sourcing and razing the natural wealth for export
to an over-populated globe in exchange for cash and
worldly goods.

The Canadians' single bond is ultimately forged
in genocide.

Canada has been built and developed and maintained
quite illegally and quite intolerably and quite repug-
nantly on top of other nations, rather than at their invitation, and without their consent or cooperation, and to
their intended demise. It is the quintessential globalist
colonial state.

The future of Canada, if allowed to unfold in its
current trajectory, will be colonial. And it will aid the
globalist colonization of the world's remaining national
and natural places.

This is a political value based on disregard for
everything except economic priorities, and possibly the
ethnic group to which one belongs, and Canadian companies operating elsewhere rely on the nearly-existent
but tractless rules of operation provided in Canada. Particularly where they fail to touch the ground on Indigenous homelands. Canada's multi-trillion dollar
international resource extraction enterprises are well-
shot of concern for human rights based liabilities. And
they've shot well over their limit of local protesters who
were unhappy at the relocation programs designed to remove them from the impending sites of gold mines, oil

pipelines, hydroelectric dams, and other such globalizing concerns.

The Canadians are content to believe in the right of the majority to benefit by the displacement, dispossession and assimilation of the minority. Canada leads by example, vigorously denying and defeating Indigenous Peoples' rights within its own hotly contested state borders; it must needs extend that denial around the world.

It's fine if Canada decides how to "reconcile" with "First Nations," while continuing to perpetrate actions of aggression, and to be in control of the waters, lands, airs, and all the revenues that accrue from use or misuse of those nations and their natural wealth. There are many states which secretly appreciate this active position. As long as Canada is loudly hazing Indigenous Peoples' rights, everyone else can carry on quietly as usual, even meekly adopting an insincerely sympathetic stance. In many cases, other countries are adopting a lot more than that from the Canadian real politik. They are adapting the Canadian "Indian Act" and the Canadian "modern day treaty process" and the Canadian "tribal council and Indian Band" systems and the Canadian Comprehensive Claims Policy; and they are particularly keen on "consultation and accommodation" – a solution to a problem created uniquely by and for Canadians.

Canada's own homegrown solution to the glaring problem of the rights of Indigenous Peoples who have never sold, ceded or surrendered their homelands to the modern day state – a problem experienced presently by every state in the western hemisphere, as well as throughout Africa, India, China, Japan, Asia, Australia, New Zealand and South America - is unmatched around the world.

Canada has unilaterally constitutionalized aboriginal rights, empowered its courts to define aboriginal rights without their meaningful participation, and qualified certain Canadians as aboriginal rights experts. The Canadian state is nothing less, according to itself, than the founder, protector, administrator and justified infringer of aboriginal rights.

Section 35 of Canada's Constitution Act, 1982, is the mechanism by which Canada has emerged as the world's leader in rubbishing Indigenous Peoples: "Aboriginal and treaty rights are hereby affirmed." It is an alternative phrasing of restraints and provisions made earlier in Canada's constitutional history – such as the Royal Proclamation of 1763, fashioned by King George III of England to quiet Pontiac's wars against Him – guaranteeing the autonomy of Indian lands not purchased outright by colonial representatives; and the Articles of Montreal, 1759 – guaranteeing Pontiac's lands in particular and freedom from molestation in general; and the British North America Act of 1867, Section 109, including that provincial powers cannot override "Other Interests." There were no Other Interests in the Dominion of Canada at that time except the Indigenous interests.

The special thing about Canada's Section 35 solution is that Canada insists it does not know what the solution is. And the Supreme Court does not know either. Any Indigenous party claiming or defending an "aboriginal right" must spend an average twenty years and $35 million in a Canadian court trying to have that right recognized as such. This allows a lot of time to carry on business as usual, and a lot of time to draft mitigating legislation to anticipate and end-run any possible outcome.

Canada was a leader in the formation of the United Nations Declaration on the Rights of Indigenous Peoples. Curious? Not very. At the eleventh hour, the draft document was gutted of the viable organs of Indigenous Peoples' rights as peoples, and it was gutted by the states which populate the UN membership. A handful of Indigenous leaders developing the Declaration, by then, owed their careers to Canadian funding. Some made a career choice to promote the gutless, degenerate form of the Declaration as an accomplishment. Others resigned.

When the vote on the UN DRIP was held in UN General Assembly, September 13, 2007, Canada threatened to withdraw International Development Aid funding from several African countries, if they did not vote against the DRIP. The African countries still voted for it. One can only suppose the African states' sympathies with the Indigenous and the hollowness of the threat.

Canada, in defense of its "no" vote, said the DRIP would undermine its substantial accomplishments in advancing Indigenous Peoples' rights. Canada said its

Indian Act, vintage 1876, and its Comprehensive Claims Policy, vintage 1976, and its Constitution Act, 1982, were superior guarantees. That is, of "Aboriginal rights" – they didn't say Canada's set-up was a better guarantor of Indigenous Peoples' rights. Canada's proposal, in a nutshell, is that states and their courts should decide what rights Indigenous Peoples have and do not have, even as the state occupies a position of conflicting interest as it supports the colonizing population with the spoils, or despoliation, of Indigenous lands gotten by deciding the Indigenous have less rights. Because each individual state knows best how to "take care of" the peoples of the land where it is, and generalized human rights would not be helpful.

This is "colonialism." Singled out as contrary to world peace and therefore a practice the sooner to be abandoned, at least in the Charter of the United Nations, it is perpetuated here and its new mechanisms are exported abroad. The expectations in a colonial situation do not include the consent of the colonized. The realities, under colonialism, don't include land-based rights, such as if your name comes from an ancestor who lived 6,000 years ago in the same place where your family lives now: that doesn't really affect how decisions are made there or who gets to live there on your family lands. Even if your family was part of an ancient alliance that cultivated, protected, and exclusively relied on that country, and even if your country never made treaty with British or Canadian colonizers. Decisions are going to be made in English, some in French, but decisions are not going to be made in the language of the land in question.

Decisions are going to be made by Governors, and Lieutenant Governors, and viceroys. And Corporate Executive Officers and banks. And then those are going to be laundered through democratic elections to appear as decisions made by the Canadian people.
Canadians have a few problems resulting from this. The phrase "the Canadian people" is a contradiction in terms. Because the present state was forged out of entrepreneurs and their refugee or indentured labour force, and it never was integrated or anchored (or legitimized) in the existing nations' civil and political frameworks, because those – and the other essential facets of those peoples – were criminalized and denied. There is now no chance for a Canadian people.

"Peoples" can absorb newcomers – like if a Mohawk person marries into the Haida nation, that person and their children could become part of the Haida people. The Haida are a people. But a "people" share a history, culture, language, identity, and lands – which Canadians do not.

Hypothetically, if the colonially constructed borders along the straight-edged provinces came down, the refugee settlers might be able to join original nations and peoples, learn the language and become citizens. At the moment there are only "original" peoples here. There is not a "Canadian people," by any definition other than the Canadian one – which beggars the definition of "a people."

It makes life complicated. When there is an election for government, and politicians pepper the roadways with little signs announcing their candidacy, even the names of the candidates have to be written in the alphabet of the language of that ethnic minority the candidate wishes to represent. Local radio, newspaper and television are all available in many languages which are not one of the state's official languages. And they are not translations of the state's "Canadian Broadcasting Corporation;" they are forms of media which serve the different communities as they are, with their unique interests competing with the interests of the other communities. A significant number of citizens do not speak French or English to conduct their business or civil or social affairs. A significant number of households do not organize their economic participation in the state in accordance with the economic structure of the state, but in accordance with the economic life of their religious center. There is no single fair and proportionate system of taxation which would blanket all the different types of households and communities and produce equal results – that's how diverse Canadians are.

And there is no general agreement on binding moral and legal principles. The various Canadian communities have no allegiance to and less love for each other. Everyone over the age of forty grew up hardly ever having seen any of the others they now call neighbours, and had only learned of them in government propaganda as the soldiers of the axes of evil; in National Geographic as colourful inhabitants of lost worlds; in films as caricatures; on the front cover of newspapers as the enemy in the current war; as the perennial infidel. The idea that everyone should live here together in sympathetic harmony was never announced as a formal social clarification, there was no accompanying national re-education program, and few are equipped for the immediate requirements of the suddenly and exponentially pluralistic environment. "Multiculturalism" programs landed like "be a tourist in your own town" advertising pamphlets.

Canadians are unique in the world for their ignorance of the concept of international law. It's not promoted, and often not reflected in the Canadian criminal code. Coming from either refugee or despotic backgrounds themselves, perhaps few Canadians ever appreciated the application of international law – or any kind of human-rights based law – and that's why they left home in the first place. However, it makes for a state where teachers, police officers, judges and politicians have not had any of the internationally-prescribed training about those rights. Neither they nor the average Canadian is aware, for instance, that the rights of Indigenous Peoples are not meant to be optional, or decided by a majority vote. The average Canadian believes that Indigenous Peoples, and their nations, will have to let go of their land claims, their culture, their traditional economies and religious practices, if that is what a majority of Canadians decide.

Canadians do not accept that this form of tyranny is a violation of very real rights of self-determination, land rights, and rights not to be victims of genocide.

Canadians are deprived, in their ignorance, of being lawful citizens of the world themselves, and will continue to deprive decent Indigenous human beings from repairing their peoples in all their civil, political, economic, social and cultural forms. Canadians continue to bulldoze, dynamite, mine, pollute, clearcut, dam, and develop the places where Indigenous sovereignty lives: in sacred places, in Indigenous homelands, where the people and their Creators talk. And Canadians continue to drain the world of the benefit of these Peoples' cosmovision and all. The victims are everyone. It is not possible to be complicit in genocide and be a proper human being.

While colonialism is singled out by the United Nations Charter as reprehensible, yet the General Assembly of the United Nations looks on as Canada perseveres in it. While that calls into question the true nature and purpose of the UN, and the reality of international courts, it does nothing to aid the Canadians or their oppressed hosts. Will the UN Charter, and human nature, amputate that limb which describes and condemns colonization? Or will "colonialism" be redefined, still leaving the fact of it to lie on the books under another name?

What is the alternative future? Either we have this imperial warehouse of satellite populations from around the world, all competing for resources and powers made possible by the state, or the colony breaks up along the original nations' lines that their gods designed. And the refugees can put their talents, and the proceeds of their camps, at the disposal of the nations they actually live in.

A $20 Blueberry

It doesn't seem to be the farmer's fault; it's definitely not the picker's fault; it's possibly not the grocery store's fault; it's – cautiously and indulgently – not the consumer's fault; but something is wrong. What is it? This society is extravagantly unwilling to feed itself, and must either import farm labour or buy produce from countries without labour standards. What is that? Is food so cheap in other countries? The old admonishment for talking about things which don't concern us – everything plus the price of rice in China – is obsolete. Incidentally, rice in Mexico is a tenth the cost of what it is here. But it comes from the same place.

People might be interested to get out their calculator and follow along at the meaningful public subsidies to every farmer, subsidies which triple the grocery store price tag on a lot of meats, fruit and vegetables. Without calculating the subsidies to farmers who only export their products. Some sort of nationalization scheme might appear from the receipts.

This is not a quantitative study, but an interested comment on substantially revealing aspects of the cost of food production in left coast Canada. There are plenty of TED talks and scientific papers – where I checked some of my curiosities – to show absurdities like the net import of apples and pears, while those are the main fruits the southern strip is best for growing; and we export them as well as importing them. This speech has also a few detailed questions and comparisons concerning the actual food production capacity of a place that is mostly mountain peak or alpine plateau, and historically was home to less than a million people - not four million people. A similar observation could be extrapolated around the globe, but generalizations don't serve.

The four thousand dollar cow

Working as a gardener for a living, I've encountered some interesting back-eddies of the food production and subsidy cycle. On one of the properties where I work, ten acres, the owners have an arrangement to let the fields to a neighbouring farmer for grazing his cattle. He brings in eight cows – four mothers and four heifers – and they eat the grass for about six months of the year. This arrangement entitles the property owners to about $4,000 in tax credits, annually. Just rounding things out, that's $500-a-head in public subsidy, and these cows haven't had a shot of penicillin or eaten a bag of grain yet. The cattle farmer himself, and the grain farmer, enjoy tax relief as well. So does the veterinarian.

One of those heifers, now valued at well over a thousand dollars in less tax revenue, is sold at auction for about a dollar a pound, averaging current prices across Canada. The heifer weighs a little less than a thousand pounds. Our free-ranging heifer, unusual in the world of stockyards, is in competition with the less costly stock yard cows. She's worth more to the tax payer, but that isn't a factor at auction. What her mother is worth, one can only guess by checking her teeth? But the mother's life is protected only to raise heifers, so we should add her annual subsidy on to each heifer she bears.

Along with the incentives to let cows graze the fields, a property with farm tax status is entitled to write off capital expenditures which the rest of the population could never even consider. A million dollars' worth of home and barn improvements might net the landlord 80% of the outlay in tax break. (The new house is for the horse-minder, and the barn is for the cows (horses).)

Farm tax status can be achieved by any property showing, correctly or very hypothetically, a $2,500 annual income from agricultural product. Someone on one acre with a dozen chickens and a couple of apple trees can get farm tax status – they may just be charging a lot for those eggs and apples. In order to produce the value of the subsidy, they would have to be moving over 40 dozen eggs a week – they can't do that with less than 20 chickens laying eggs almost every day. Which is unlikely, but keeping a chicken is the cost of eggs. The chicken has to be, ahem, replaced, every two and a half years.

A closer look at that. The chicken eats a little under a hundred dollars' worth of food over the year. ($2,000 for food for the chickens, in keeping with our scenario subsidy exam.) She needs some space to run around and shelter, but she doesn't need heat. She needs water and she would very much prefer some green grass, clover, dandelions and kitchen scraps. (Apparently, some "farmers" have managed to get all that – the sunshine, the greens, the variety kitchen scrap, and the special habitat – into a pill; so they can raise three thousand chickens in one barn and get them to lay maximum yield. Or at least that's what people who buy eggs at $3/dozen might be telling themselves.)

The cost of everything but the chicken itself, the grain, the chicken shack and the fencing, a few necessities like a good rain jacket and boots and a few tools, and possibly a few rounds of anti-mite powder, is a matter of elbow grease: collecting the eggs, feeding and watering the chickens; maintaining the shack and the fence; the redistribution of leftovers from the kitchen; and organizing the sale of the eggs. So in this example, the small land owner who works elsewhere and just keeps up the chickens for - whatever their reasons are, "we" have produced five hundred dozen eggs in a year. It cost us about $2,500 in public tax break subsidy, which the farmer used to pay the grain supplier, coat and boots store, the vet, etc. It then cost the consumer $5/dozen, or another $2,500. This is the $10 dozen. In other words, without the government tax subsidy, the farmer would have had to charge $10/dozen to make a profit of $2,500 over the year. And that's not a lot of money for a job that can't be shirked lest the chickens starve and the egg supply dries up.

But it is a lot of money if the public is matching consumer spending dollar-for-dollar on food. And the trouble comes when the tax-break-receiving landowner is not really producing 500 dozen eggs, but a few dozen.

Agricultural tax incentives to people who can afford any kind of a land base are so… interesting… that property

owners in the Okanagan are razing orchards and slap-
ping up (doomed) vineyards because of a swing in the
government mood toward a British Columbia wine fad.
The incentives are available to people who have demon-
strated that they cannot grow a grape, much less make a
decent vinegar – to say nothing of wine.

In fact, one lucky owner of an older vineyard won a
bit of a lottery. Fire destroyed the place, so the state agriculture department decided to replace the whole thing:
rebuild and plant again. The owner had no interest in the
grapes, but he certainly sold the place at a handsome
profit.

So there are the grape vines, and there are the, ah,
receipt books, to prove that land is a contributing member of food security. The original orchard really was producing a lot of food – but the "farmer" is not really
interested in all the fuss (and expense and uncertainty)
of getting the fruit to market.

Local Fruit
According to a Quebecois picker, the workplace environment at an orchard is live-in. It takes a week or two
to pick a big apple orchard, and, ideally, there will be
pears and plums to pick over the weeks before and after,
too. The camping arrangement for the pickers at an
Okanagan orchard in 2015 featured one water tap – cold;
one outhouse; and seventy pickers in their own tents,
cooking meals on their portable propane stoves.

People on welfare out east come this way for the
summer, collect their cheques back home and sublet

their places, like on a holiday. They can camp in the orchard fields and use the money they make picking to entertain themselves – possibly at Anarchist Book Fairs on Vancouver Island – before going home for winter.

The Quebecois picker was curious about the life of his employers, as they were originally from India, and he knows a little about Indian spirituality and the economic and social caste system that influences things on the subcontinent. He asked, what kind of caste would the picker be in, in India? He was informed that he would occupy a very low spot in the caste scheme. This was perhaps confirmed to him in more real, place-based terms when he witnessed a helicopter launched off its house-side pad to dry the cherries when it rained just before harvest. Surely the helicopter is one of the more expensive farm implements in use today.

At an attracting and obviously misleading rate of pay of $11.35 hourly, estimated and advertised online by the very unlikely algorithm which estimates a fruit picker's annual salary in BC at just over $22,000 dollars (fruit is only harvested a few months of the year – there's not enough hours of daylight there for that annual income. In fact, if you worked every day for three months for ten hours a day you would earn $10,000. But what you would pay transporting yourself to all those farms, and if you got the best steady first pick every time – which is what that wage is based on – your costs would substantially undermine the gross.), the actual rate of pay is by piece work: $18.06 / bin (27.1 cu. ft.) That's eighteen dollars per twenty seven cubic feet of apples picked.

But it is not only whiffy dreadlocked hippies who subsidize the fruit producers of BC via the welfare system of Canada.

From the beginning, berry picking is political. Some families, or labour crews, get the first pick; others get second and worse. The "first pick" is the only hope anyone has of making a decent wage, whether raspberries or blueberries: the fruit is abundant and it falls off the canes and bushes without resistance, by the copious handful.

It becomes further political when you go on in and take a look at the next bunch, who are picking raspberries for $5 per flat. After the first pick, a worker is searching the canes and bushes for ripe – not rotten, green or mouldy – fruit, and the berries are picked one or two at a time. It takes an hour to fill a flat of raspberries after the first pick is done, and a flat is worth $5 to the piece-work picker. Well, it takes a good picker an hour to pick a flat of raspberries in the second pick. To say nothing of the third.

Some of those pickers are homeless locals and they sleep in the fields. This is not hard to assess at 7am on site. The homeless will still be homeless in January, and the public will afford them as best they can, under the unfriendly government circumstances, to feed and shelter and clothe them.

After the first pick, then the youth soccer teams, disabled people with community-access social workers (supervised and transported and housed by public subsidy), the pensioners, the single mothers with five kids; then they all are admitted to come and work for $5/hour. They, along with the homeless people, are heavily subsidized by state welfare programs; family allowance; public school.

So why is the farm privately owned, when every aspect of its operation is purchased by the state, eighty cents on the dollar?

If farmers had to pay all their workers minimum wage, what would a blueberry cost? About $20. So the only way people can afford to eat food grown in the country is when the remaining $19.90 of that cost is socialized.

What is the residual observation, once we notice that we can't afford to feed ourselves? When we do, it looks like this:

There is a cow in Lillooet whose milk is sold at $7/L ($28/G) and a meat chicken that is sold at $5/lb. The farmers who raise them are not subsidized, they also do not pay anyone's wages – they feed the cow and milk the thing and feed the chicken and butcher it by themselves as part of their daily chores – and then go off and hold down a full time job. What they get out of it is enough milk and chicken meat for themselves, that is their total return. But they own the land those animals live on, they are often raising the animal's food – or half of it, they are not making improvements to their facilities because of tax rebates, but they don't hire anyone, but they usually volunteer in the community,

Hand over fist taxation and subsidy
First the sack of grain seed is taxed, as it is sold to the farmer who grows the next crop of it. All the machinery is taxed on purchase, and a meaningful amount of farm machinery is bought with government money in subsidies. A little tractor costs $15,000, and that can be bought with a variety of government grants. That farmer, who bought the grain and the machinery and paid tax and received subsidy, receives a hefty annual income tax rebate. The farmer also buys pesticides and fertilizers, and pays tax on those.

Note: The farmer lives on the outskirts of a Fraser Valley city, down a narrow, poorly paved road about two kilometers from a main road. But that "main road" is the major artery connecting the farms to the city and highway. The tractors and farm machinery that travel it are hard on the pavement, and often very muddy, and City employees maintain it with publicly funded vehicles, equipment and wages.

When the distributor of the farmer's crop buys it, she pays tax. When she resells it, her customers pay tax again on the same product. When the chickens those customers raised on that grain are sold to another distributor, tax is paid. When the consumer buys it in the grocery store, tax is paid again. If it's going to a restaurant, the diner pays tax again.

Everyone who worked in that production chain for their wages then pays income tax.

More City workers collect the compost.

Apparently, federal subsidies to agriculture were as high as $5.4 billion in 1987, as low as $524 million in 1995, and in 2009 amounted to $922 million. But the information is just not disaggregated. Was that $1b in direct "I'll buy that for you" handout?

A little blueberry

Late in August, 2017, I counted fifty people in a blueberry field. It's on the other side of the fence, down the slope, from the vineyard I work at, and it's not very big. Maybe two acres. The main blueberry harvest had occurred weeks earlier, and in my prying and visiting and questioning at that time, I learned that the heat of this summer had made the pick a rather urgent affair.

Blueberries are native to the Lower Mainland and indeed up the coast aways. They thrive with cedar litter around their bases; that's where they grow – at the dappled edges of cedar forests. Industrial farmers from Richmond to Chilliwack have now cultivated them by the tens of thousands of acres, without a tree in view. Suffice to say they are vulnerable to full sun in a heat wave.

My observation is that there were very few blueberries to be picked in that late August field. My extrapolation is that the pickers, all wearing typical Indian (or Pakistani?) garb, would have had no chance of making $10 – at $0.40/pound – during the two hours they were there. But those were the conditions. Those pickers don't get to pick the conditions. I had always thought it odd that the chain link fences had three rows of barbed wire on top.

One morning at the end of July I had a rocky start to the day. Because of the smoke in the air – there was an air quality advisory on, due to about a million acres of forest on fire. I had gotten from bed into the truck in little more than one movement. I was hungry and so I drove through a fast food option. The result was truly dreadful – a stale bagel housing an egg with a grey yolk and a slice of tomatoe that was half stem. Luckily I had the luxury of rejecting the circumstances as they were – I was hungry and I didn't want to do four hours of vine twisting on an empty stomach – so I drove back up to the restaurant and got a new breakfast sandwich. But by that time I would be starting my work in the vineyard almost 45 minutes later than was ideal, if I wanted to get four hours in and avoid the stifling heat and the full smoke.

On my way to the vineyard, at 6:30 am, I had passed several busloads of farm workers. I decided to follow up with them, pursuing this question of the cost of food, instead of twisting grape vines. I stopped in at home and picked up my camera.

The scenes I caught with my camera that morning were sort of apocalyptic. I stopped on the roadside and photographed a team of mostly Mexican workers against a backdrop of a dusty gravel quarry, an ashen sky, and a red sun rising. The air quality advisory for that day indicated a "Fine Particulate Matter" count for the Fraser

Valley, including where we were, that recommended the very young and the very old should stay indoors.

I asked around at the landscape supply place at some point in that week why the grounds guy, outside, wasn't wearing a mask? Because only a mask as sophisticated as would strain gas would have been effective. None of the pickers were wearing masks of any sort. I took pictures of some "very old" people out there at work. They were wearing turbans, alongside their baseball-cap-wearing coworkers.

Instead of fleeing the scene of my totally invasive photography session, I decided to make small talk and small lies. I said I was just there to get photos for the news. Okay? My Spanish is not fluent, but we got through it. One of the strawberry pickers was a lot closer to me than the others. I asked him, "Trabajan conjuntos, ustedes?" He explained that they don't usually work together, just that day, and that the workers there were from different parts of Mexico. They didn't come here together. I asked him, "Y, como es todo?" (And how is everything?) Well, communication is 80% body language anyway. He didn't need to say a thing. And the words he did say contradicted the other 80% of the message.

I was by no means finished my investigation, but I was finished there.

I turned down a road I had seen a busload of people take when I was on my way back with my breakfast bagel. There they were, at the end of the road. It was a blueberry field. Ramsey was at the side of the road. As I slowed down to park my truck, rolling down the window and making a greeting out of a smile, he showed a very outgoing cheerfulness. I pulled up on the side of the road and asked if I could park there for a minute. A full-size school bus was parked opposite me, so it left little room for anyone to drive in to the end of the road and turn around. Ramsey said it was fine. Another man with him, dressed and groomed immaculately, remained silent and pointedly aloof.

Upon closer observation, which I engaged at Ramsey's generous invitation, the chasm between Ramsey's presentation and that of the silk-clad fellow was legendary. I only thought about it later. The other fellow was manicured: beard, turban, fingernails; smart shoes; creaseless and immaculate garments. He could have been going to a wedding. At least, a wedding in my family. Ramsey was filthy.

I was also filthy, or dressed in ragged jeans and T-shirt that were imminently to become filthy. I told Ramsey I was on the way to work, but was curious about the opportunities afforded by picking blueberries. He told me that you get $0.40/pound for the blueberries. I then confessed I had other work which competed successfully with that wage. How much could one person earn, picking blueberries? "Oh, some can pick 150 pounds in a day," he told me. "Some 200." Given the fact that Ramsey could not walk down the shoulder of the road to the level of the blueberry field without assistance, I guessed that he would not be picking anywhere near that amount.

He sat on an overturned bucket, tucked into the bushes, to pick. I decided to pick into his second bucket while we talked.

Wasn't my persistence rewarded. Ramsey had graduated from a college in India, only to then discover his skin was too dark to get a job commensurate with his education. He explained that he came from the east of India, or at least that was an explanation which I do not understand, but he offered the information as an explanation. So he emigrated to Canada, to BC.

He told me he lives, and has lived for a few years, on the property of the fellow (the nicely dressed one aforementioned) he works for. He told me that fellow is a very generous man, to let him pick close to the road so he doesn't have to go far. Ramsey has terrible arthritis in his feet. Apparently he takes some kind of drug treatment for the pain and inflammation, but that's it. He has a daughter. He's divorced. He's about 75 years old. He doesn't have a phone number or an e-mail address.

Incidentally, there is only an outside window of one week's worth of blueberry picking, the first pick, during which one could pick over a hundred pounds of blueberries in a day. After that, it's a much less productive activity – battling the little leaves falling into the bucket, and twisting only a few berries from each bunch instead of a handful.

It's interesting to balance my account of the blueberry picking with the details of the field I was working in that day: three acres of vineyard grapes, apple trees and plum trees which all dropped their fruit on the ground in accordance with the absentee landlord's wishes just to keep the vines and trees up and retain future resale property value. My kid and I picked as much as we could, as often as we could, and took it to the food bank. A few hundred pounds each of apples, plums and grapes.

I went home to a rented two bedroom condo, and Ramsey to a small room in a row of small cabins.

Trout fishing, or, "there's plenty of wilderness left"
A lot of BC is steep and rocky mountainside. A lot of it is alpine mountain top, and sub-alpine plateau. A good strip of it is rocky, salty coastline. The most agriculturally suitable areas have been mostly developed into human housing, shopping malls, auto malls, highways, industrial parks, acres of greenhouses, and electrical transmission lines. Remaining delta lands, once rich black earth and marsh, are now nearly sterile under the heavy chemical saturation of industrial agriculture.

The mainstay of this area was historically salmon: a hundred million sockeye going up the Fraser River at the height of a four year cycle. That natural bounty has been reduced to one percent. It was also moose, deer, migratory birds, and thousands of species of fish and water mammals that lived in valley bottoms and marshes. Those areas have been dammed… replaced with cows… clearcut.

Blueberries are grown in premium agricultural areas, in the Fraser Valley, where almost anything could be grown. And we export 75% of those blueberries to

Quebec and Ontario, USA, and now China.

I am personally responsible for wiping out a rainbow trout population. Human beings are too big for their britches, even at the age of ten. I will never forget baiting the last big trout in the beaver pond. I wasn't to know that it was the last, but it was the last one I ever caught, and that is a good indication. I definitely did not know that I was wiping them out. Between the time I started fishing there, about age seven, and the time I got the last trout at about age twelve, all the trout ponds – which are essentially beaver dams – within five miles had been thrashed by clearcut logging. They were full of silt and only sixteen inches of water remained on top; the beavers moved away because there wasn't a tree standing anywhere near their creeks; and gone were the moose that used to gently till the sedge marshes between ponds, where they ate the rare herbs they needed. Also the farmers' cattle ranges included all the bottom land, so the cows butchered a lot of creek bed spawning areas by crossing on the gravel. One of our downstream neighbours blew a hole in the top-most dam, to improve his water supply.

That last fish was probably nesting when I discovered it in the creek below the dam. Over a few years, I had caught all the mature trout. And when it came to this last, I was driven by a force more dangerous than hunger: the quest for glory. My identity rested on continuing to catch bigger trout than anyone else. I baited it for ages, casting my lures and flys and worms in front of it.

Eventually it bit.

Nobody ever told me I should leave some to produce the next generation of the species.
But the point is that a ten year old can wipe out a population of fish, and even the most modest, modern thinking farms, are taking a disproportionate bite out of their environment. Farming goats and chickens? Goodbye lynx, bobcat, cougars. Farming hay on the Fraser benches? Hello massive water diversion from already arid benchland, and goodbye deer. That used to be the deer's summer dining room – but a lot of farmers shoot them there now. Enough that the deer know better than to go back.

The examples of local life extinction are innumerable, never to be counted. The examples of how profoundly a single rebounding species amplifies the life around it are, very sadly, far fewer; but undeniably illuminating. Now that sea otters are returning in greater numbers, they are catalyzing the populations of dozens of plant, fish and bird species on the coast. For instance, the red and orange billed oyster catchers aren't really very good oyster catchers at all: they are oyster-bits scavengers, and they follow the otters around to get their scraps. They can't dive deep enough to get the anemones, oysters, clams they rely on. The otters get them, eat them on the surface of the bays and inlets, and the leftovers float away to become the sea birds' first course. Kelp forests have regenerated as the otters farm them, digging up the ocean floor for kelp roots to spread easily, and propagating kelp all the while.

Examples of the continuing and intensifying plunder of ecosystems abound. The food export industry of BC is sacrificing the wild salmon for an easy harvest of farmed Atlantic salmon – competing with and infecting the wild salmon in their own migration routes - which is exportable to consumers abroad who know no better than to eat it because it's cheap.

Farm size

Back to my youth: there was a community of twenty households spread over 70 miles of dirt road, field and canyon, which formed a loose-knit, actually often unravelling, hamlet of cowboys, hippies and Indians. Many of the cowboy and Indian families were tenant farmers working on the cattle ranches and hayfields. The hippies were tending crops which did not contribute anything to anyone's food needs, but they were permanent residents along with the Indians who still lived on their ancestral lands and had suffered to swallow the pill of enfranchisement, in refusing to move to an Indian reserve, and losing Indian Status; and many of the ranchers were either mixed families or were themselves responsible for clearing the fields of previously resident Indians with gunfire. There were draft dodgers and a few retired couples "getting away from it all," and the one-room school teacher's family.

Before the area was logged out, these people participated in an annual hunter's and trapper's feast. They brought their own specialties and shared them around:

cougar balls; moose and deer meat; bear sausage; and things so unlikely I've forgotten what they were. After the area was logged out and the ungulates subsequently shot out by hunters from the city with quads on logging roads, this event ceased to be held. Hunting guides had a few years left, taking more intrepid city slickers to the backs of the mountains for the last big deer and bighorn sheep. There they did what I did to the trout in our beaver pond.

As to the twenty families of that time, all but four were permanently displaced by changes in food production. Motorcycles replaced the cowboys and their horses. The price of beef dropped to a level that made the remuneration for raising it – even when it was subsidized by vast ranges of grassland for six months of the year – half of what the process cost. Ginseng replaced hay in the fields of the Thompson region, for the Chinese and Korean markets, and the price of hay doubled within a year. Hobbyists with small planes and helicopters bought out some of the more beautiful, but bankrupt, ranches and replaced the livestock with airstrips, faux conceits such as Buddhist-style shrines amid hot tubs and massage parlours, and guest accommodation for the very rich. Less wealthy city folk bought other ranches and turned a profit on cycling humans through their guest cabins rather than sheep through the paddocks. The Alberta stock yards made their mark thus.

The vast majority of the farmland, which was just cultivated hayfields, was consolidated under the ownership of a rich farmer from the Fraser Valley who brought in labour for the minimum of the season: to produce the golden hay. And he padlocked the gates across roads which led to areas that previously had been part of the larger community. No one who grew up in that hamlet lives there now.

And all the while, food came from further and further away. Food got less nutritious, more preserved and processed, and more expensive.

"Feed the world"

Were we wrong to join Bob Geldof's anthem in 1985? If the song had been more specifically titled, we might have thought twice: "feed all the human beings as cheaply as possible at the expense of all other life." He could have added a verse about increasing farmland by bulldozing wetlands and wiping out amphibious species and migratory birds; draining small lakes and straightening winding rivers which previously produced all kinds of fish and fowl – again, for flat farmland; eventually building acres of electricity-dependent greenhouses over that farmland; watering the plateau hayfields from the rivers and fertilizing with the salmon fry that came in the pipes with the water; monocropping with berries bound for export and flushing those thousands of acres of valley-bottom with chemical pesticides and fertilizers and fungicides – to the complete extinction of resident insects and birds; caging millions of mammals in high-density one-stop slaughter houses that produced such bafflingly large amounts of toxic effluent that no one can bring themselves to admit the problem; and those sorts of things.

And it would have been more honest if there had been a verse about how the money to buy food, now that huge amounts of food production land were busy growing crops for peoples elsewhere, would be raised by taking such measures as converting orchards to vineyards for cash to buy food from elsewhere. And possibly some sort of extrapolated insight about such inevitable results as high-mountain Andean farms being reduced to agricultural factories to raise their beloved and ancient high protein quinoa crops for export because they can no longer afford to eat it.

At the extreme opposite end of the spectrum, here, people pay $5 for a handful of leaves of chard or kale at a Farmers' Market that is only open three hours a week.

Hungry?
People can be very tetchy about the idea of nationalizing assets, or, in this case, repossessing assets which have been lent out as livelihoods for some time. The first person I mentioned this idea to, seeing as how we already subsidize everything in our groceries dollar-for-dollar, or more, she replied: "But how would people be motivated if they just had a government job to grow our food? We might not get any food at all?"

So, the thing is, we don't want people who are motivated by money to be in charge of our food production. We want people who are crazy about frogs; people who are motivated by a wild connection to the ancient DNA in the heritage and heirloom and select varieties of plants they grow. We want people who are fascinated by worms and bacteria, and people whose bodies are just hard-wired for hard work, and people who have to be outdoors in order to be happy to live. We want people who want the lifestyle that is wanted to produce the food we want. And we want to take our families now and then, out to the farms and fields, and help them for a day or two here and there over the year. Teach our kids that this is what they are made of, even if we do live in a city.

just among the crowd

LETTER TO AUNTIE JEAN

Written on January 29th of 2014 in response to her Christmas letter, this message was never posted and my Auntie Jean died in care near her home in Barnstaple, Devon, on July 22, 2014. Jean Woodhams was a journalist, like her father my great uncle Arthur Thain. She was the first person to whom I mailed my newly published book, The Colonial Present, *and due to her fierce and tender and tireless and discriminating love, she has become a voice on my Central Committee.*

Dear Auntie Jean,

I am at long last having a truly "Dear Auntie Jean" moment! I think of you often but, alas, much more seldom are the moments in which I actually have the time and space to drop a line. I suppose this one is yet less than perfect – the only materials presenting are this crummy lined notebook and slow old pen. Never mind.

Got your Xmas letter with the usual delight! So lovely to hear from you. I appreciate very much that you imagine my uses and the life of my book which has just begun. It was an exciting start, being able to have fifty copies of the thing while in New York last May. For the third time I attended the Permanent Forum on Indigenous Issues and was able to witness the stories of travesty and triumph from around the world, as well as to meet so many exceptional people. With the help of a friend who has given me a place to stay these last years, in Queens, Brooklyn and now the Bronx, I was able to give three talks on the book and the situation in Canada. One was televised and the other two – no three, four altogether – to very sympathetic and dynamic listeners.

I am convinced that NYC should have its own international borders, perhaps like the Vatican City, as a sort of cathedral of people from every place on the globe. Suffice to say the visit was busy and productive.

Afterwards my travelling was extended to Geneva, UN HQ, for the unlikely phenomenon of a thing called the Expert Mechanism on the Rights of Indigenous Peoples. We were drawn to the occasion of their report on means of access to justice for Indigenous Peoples. That's what they call the Líl'wat now, where I married in, an "Indigenous People." Since Eala's dad died, our relatives launched a petition in 2007 with this NGO which included the complaint that neither Canada nor British Columbia has jurisdiction over their children – particularly the indiscriminate removal of their children to foster families far away. You can only imagine.

This petition has very recently been admitted to the Commission, the Inter-American Commission on Human Rights! In fact, only five days ago. Our general elation is hard to convey.

But back to the book: I was able to disperse it to people who took it home to at least two dozen countries. That is really the exciting bit I set out to tell.

Here at home the publisher is very stingy with her assistance, apparently even failing to print the thing in bulk and have it available to booksellers. She begins her response to my complaint with, "Well you have to understand about the publishing industry…". And after all that I am finding it difficult to have the book reviewed. Oh well. It is "out there," available online and so on. I can only take refuge in the thought that many writers were never taken on until they were well and truly out of the way!

As for myself, I am happy to advise that I have found a wonderful home in a 107 year old house that has a great back porch. If I recall, you were a smoker once! One requires a back porch in order to carry on such vices today. And the lucky thing is that my flat is the middle one, where upstairs and down come to carry out their social business. There is the great company and great wine, and an occasional half bottle of undrunk wine left over in my fridge. More than I can afford, often enough, but this writer should never be far from her cigarettes and wine, or good company – the latter of which here in the house includes folk from Brittany, Australia, New Zealand, California and the Gulf Islands.

Since the book, it is my hope to publish a collection of short stories. I have many, but completion is the thing. I've just noticed that there are accumulating a few typos and possibly incomprehensible text. I hope your eye is still trained to receive the hand-written word – so many are not!

As I write this by candle light on my back porch, Auntie Jean, when will I get to see you again? I think I conveyed my attempts to get to Exeter via Geneva, but those were inconceivable.

It is impossible for me to hire a fare across the Atlantic, never mind first across the North American continent, to visit you. This is the duress into which every colonial subject is born. I cannot afford to come home. One of the points I labour over in my book is that there were cheap fares to N America from Europe, but none whatsoever in the opposite direction. Many posters were stenographed to lure GB subjects away across the sea; none were authored to advise people of ship routes home again. You can approximate the dilemma. The traffick was headed away from Europe. Why? To colonize new lands and send the riches home, not the people. I feel very undone. As most from Ireland in 1847 must have felt.

Wishing only for the impossible, to see you soon, I send my love.

Kerry

Letter sent to Auntie Jean's memorial service,

This is what I want to say for Auntie Jean as we remember her together.

Last July I went on a fairly sudden and unexpected trip to Geneva. It struck me that Geneva is not so far from Barnstaple, and so I tried to find a flight from Exeter. I investigated helicopter travel from London to Barnstaple; bus routes, rail and so on. But the flight from Exeter to Geneva, if I had got there from London, would cost about five thousand pounds and involve three days of flights which connected in five different countries.

On hearing the news that Auntie Jean had graduated from this world I explained through my tears to my daughter that I wished then I had become an oil profiteer, or a uranium miner, or a warlord or any type of godforsaken but profitable vocation - if it only meant that I could afford to have gone to see Auntie Jean one more time. I'm not sure that the few letters I sent her over the years really conveyed to her how special she is to me.

Even though the truth is I have only spent a handful of days in her company, Auntie Jean's voice is on my Central Committee. She is wise, cautious, slow to judge, and keenly insightful. After that, she was quite determined and fearless. Her love and tenderness for Uncle John, who I nearly killed with some strong plum sauce while they were visiting here at the ranch, was illuminating. She has inspired me with an understanding of good grace which I can only try to achieve. So few people practice it the way she did. I recall that about her presence, which is vivid in my memory, even from when I met her as a child in England.

Her career as a journalist gave me courage to write - because it had already been done! I've never read more than a few lines of what she wrote, but the fact that her dad did it and she did it somehow made a space for me to do the same. I am grateful for that and I like to think she felt my carrying on with writing made her an important link in a family tradition that continues. She gave me her "news hound," Baxter, and his special bows and accumulated Royal Rota Press passes. I will take care of him and he of me.

My daughter Eala is sixteen now, and she got to meet Auntie Jean in 2008 - many thanks to my mum who brought all of us to England and Ireland to connect with our family there. Two years ago I decided to add something to Eala's name which had unfortunately not occurred to me when she was born: Jean, and I got to tell Auntie Jean about this on the phone. She was happy with that.

Auntie Jean will live in my heart as long as it pumps blood. She will live with me in my being forever more -

as we always have. At times like this I have to insist on a timeless togetherness, a spiritually tractable meaning in our earthly lives, that lets me never be far from her.

Thank you all so much for getting together to share in our love and appreciation for Jean. I miss her terribly and pray for her safe travels. God bless you.

THE CRUTCHES

After a painful lapse of the hip's usual flexion and platform functions, resulting in an inability to walk, a pair of crutches is the sweet kiss of liberty. I can move! I can propel myself forward into the world!

Without crutches I would be immobile. Unable to visit the café, the post office, the festival, the doctor; unable to walk down the street.

When others look at me they see the crutches first, and sometimes nothing else. They see a handicap, not the technology of liberation; not a person with an enabling device; not a soul set free. And that is an absolutely backwards view.

There are other types of crutches which people cannot see past to the person that is set loose by them. A cross worn around the neck wards off skeptics as well as demons: some people cannot embrace a person who is enlivened and made whole by their confidence in Christ. Christ's presence symbolized gives the necklace-wearer courage, it satisfies the deep-tissue vocal chords of fear which would otherwise nag them back behind their front door. Anyone who does not rest some broken part of themselves on the Bible only sees a shackle hanging like a noose when they see that pendant. It is not the shackle but the key that frees that individual, day after day, to go out and love. Their dependence is at once their liberation.

Some witnesses of others notice only the skunky reek of marijuana on those addicts who need to sedate oversensitive parts of themselves in order to function at a common denominator. The humble, happy person before them, however, is just a cripple, even a degenerate.

When the red face and hard kerosene breath of the alcoholic present themselves forward of other personal attributes, some others see only a rubby. They close their ears to the poetry that spills across the open threshold of the soul made bold by spirits. But if not for those fortifying draughts, the very feeling person might languish behind the bars of insecurity, inhibition and uncertainty - stuck behind their precious gift of vulnerability, and the caged bird's song would never leave to musicalize a garden or set fire to a protest rally or grieve in loud ballads that unlock others' ceremonial wailing.

And the cloud of tobacco. All four of my grandparents were addicts. The smoke undid binding social constructs that constricted conversation to automated subjects which propelled them along newspaper headlines. After the Second World War there was too much to talk about; so much and so meaningful it was that people found it hard to talk at all. The second great war had entirely altered everyone in Europe's life entirely. My grandparents lived in Britain. And no one discussed the changes, but employed that legendarily stiff upper British lip.

The common people, the poor people like my grandparents who had provided very replaceable fodder for the Great War, could not sort what made for acceptable discussion and what didn't. Tobacco gave them courage, or knocked out their internalized critics, or forged connections between their feelings and their thoughts which had perhaps been broken. Later my grandfather took up a pipe, which suited his more leisurely days and his more considered way of enjoying a restful sit down. The others had died by then.

Why did they die? One stroke, one heart attack, and one case of cancer. They were bound to die – everybody dies. But they lived, too. They lived larger and more daring than if inhibition had been suffered to hold them back.

The world can be an unfriendly place. It doesn't hurt to have a friend alongside, even if it's a half-conscious pseudo-spiritual one. A friend that can be bought at most stores, for an affordable price. When experience has got one's tongue, especially if one is part of a low-class of citizenry such as would be willed to say nothing, stimulants or depressants can drown out the learned reprimands and give license to the spirit.

It is hypocritical of people to condemn someone for using a crutch. Michelangelo did not work without a bottle of wine at lunch. Mozart had trouble caging his angels and demons, and was only capable of work at great intervals: intervals which were marked by the use of opiates. The foremost poets of an entire era in English literature were opium addicts. The first Prime Minister of Canada was an alcoholic.

The Special Olympics for athletic competition

would not even exist if there was not a ready under-standing of the body's vulnerability to injury; what about the chemical prosthetics required to support an injured Olympian mind? What if injury is also a fact of life?

How many offended witnesses to crutches, vices, habits, medications, use none themselves? How many can criticize and testify that they have never been made more alive by a love song, or a verse, or a cup of coffee? A pill? And if they can't testify to isolation from all the intoxicants of nature in this life, how then do they assign merit to one over another, or rationalize one means of support while condemning another?

They act as if they are the only ones who recognize that something has been compromised; that assistance is needed. They act as if the ones who lean on their crutches are somehow unaware of the fifth wheel.

When I come home from a day on crutches, there are pains under my arms, in my wrists, in my thumb joint. The crutches rub and wear. When the alcoholic goes home, or wakes up at home, or elsewhere, there is a price to be paid. Something wasn't payed. The dope smoker can't recall his dreams. The Christian feels mis-understood, in spite of everything she has done. The cig-arette butts are a smelly reminder of whatever's missing.

No one on crutches is unaware of the cost of their bridges into the world. A toll is paid every time.

SOCIAL NEEDIA

Society is a reciprocal venture.

Everyone brings something; everyone wants something. "Social" used to mean more than the present-day consumer style of purchasing other people's interest with offers of super-drama and controversy; pain-per-view and bias confirmation.

What did an individual's social needs use to be? First of all, they need something to stimulate that endorphin production. People need people. What did you make of that?! Yeah, that's what I got out of it! Or, This is what happened to me! Oh my gosh – what's that like? Or, I'm never going to forget this dance. Me neither! And so on. Good company is a relief, and it's fortifying, and it's usually the starting place for a lot of creativity.

And that's just the individual's receiving end of the social need. The society end of "social" needs the individual's commitment. In the social exchange, something should be taxed off for the greater good. But it's not as hard as all that; the social capital accrues almost effortlessly. The simple state of "being with" produces energy, courage, curiosity… engendering compassion for others and the desire to experience again the satisfaction of helping someone else, solving a problem, or asking for a hand and getting one from a stranger. Seeing a new fashion take.

We need to find out that we are not the only ones; that someone else out there is in the same place; that there are other places; that someone else has been through this place and they say there's the other side. We need catalysts. We need compassion and interest and validation, among other things. We need attention. We need a reflection. We just need help figuring out how to do something. Sometimes we need help because we haven't noticed that the thing we are doing is overwhelmingly difficult… because we are doing it wrong. We need to reproduce. The word is that becoming proficient requires a thousand hours practice – consider how long the training period is to be able to flirt and carry on a conversation with someone who takes your breath away!

We need to be heard. We need to get good at listening. We need to sort out day to day problems with others who get in the way – or don't show up.

A "social" media, to get a little more technical, actually involves a who and a what and a when and a where and a why. A properly constituted social situation, a medium you can really work with, involves – for example – people, a bus stop, a little wind, a recent event being discussed, an interruption, a question of power or status in resolving a little matter of a cat up a tree. Social skill is entirely transferable. You need the same set of skills to deal with the snobby strangers and the cat at the bus stop as you do when you walk into a city hall meeting and present on why you believe that if developers want to subsume another ten acres of forest, they should be forced to go in there and personally murder the raccoons, deer, bears, squirrels, and owls.

"Media" is another dynamic word. It can be used to describe mixed materials, such as potting soil. Here we are in the ongoing abstraction of human development, so ungrounded, our minds getting further and further from our plant-eating, water-drinking, air-breathing bodies.

If it was necessary to distinguish the internet platforms accessed by hand-held digital coms manned by individuals for their own interest as "social" – from what was that being distinguished? Maybe it's the fact that the content of the twitter tweets and the facebook faces and the instagram tags are not filtered or edited – it's kind of anarchic, no rules; it's kind of socialist in the same way freedom of the press was – you just need to have a press, or in this case iphone/data/wifi, to exercise that freedom. It's social because it's not state or church or corporate. At least, it was not state or church or corporate for about two seconds. But one wonders at the versatility of this word "social," and its use as a label on free digital platforms, and how in this context it has perhaps been misunderstood.

Were newspapers not social media? If not, how in the heck were they not? There were columns for letters to the editor; personal ads; obituaries; ads for cars, groceries and odd jobs. Maybe people think that is "corporate" media, because it was published by a member of the community who ran that publication as a business. What worries me is the presumption that individuals can somehow just lead their lives, buying their bananas and bikes and iphones, as if they were separate from that "corporate" world. That "corporate" world is actively designed, delivered, perpetuated, inceased, trafficked and made what it is by exactly that individual consumer and the people he lives among. His entire social experience is in the context of what someone else has built (including his living space) and the more he withdraws and says he is not "part of that system," the less he is anything else but a product of it, with no authorship in engineering any of his most basic survival needs, nor his unique personal needs – if he had developed personally. You're either part of society or a result of it. Nobody said it was easy.

Research shows that getting "likes" on facebook, and retweets, and youtube subscriptions, does stimulate the production of endorphins. It also stimulates the participant to make more posts along the lines of the ones they got "likes" for.

But does endorphin production really capture the social role and life of the human condition? Not if you include constructive discussion.

Can endorphins keep moving without serotonin? Can this primary neurotransmitter stay fit on a diet, ingested and processed while seated, of digital display content?

On facebook, everyone passes remark. "Write a comment." In face-to-face situations, alternatively, passing remark is not necessarily appropriate. It's gossipy. Who am I to judge? What do I know about the situation? And, perhaps more importantly, what don't I know about the situation? These kinds of considerations are not really invited by the restricted characters, the restricted attention spans of the scrolling, anonymous participant in the online stream.

The confines in which social media is conducted breed the habit of passing remark rather than communicating. In person, there would be a lot more cues as to whether it was a good time to make a comment.

It's not a myth that communication is 80% non-verbal. If social media is replacing communication, think: four people sitting at a table in a café together… staring down at their iphones and texting and scrolling and chuckling and harrumphing and occasionally twisting sideways to display their screen to their companion, what is only 20% communication going to leave us with? What do we hope will come by reducing our contact by 80%? And what about our 80% intake deficiency? For instance, interactions on social media aren't marked by event. No one says, *remember the time we were chatting online and you laughed so hard your drink came out your nose?*

80% of communication was body language, tone of voice. Does social media force us up into our heads? Without that 80% of communication, even elaborate emails from trusted friends can be misread.

What did social needs use to be? Confirmation. Affirmation. Challenge. Skepticism and debate. Argument. Doubt. Identity. Love. Companionship.

Companionship today is found by young people who interrupt their screen time (gaming, movie watching, surfing) just long enough to type a few characters to someone else online (sitting alone somewhere else staring at another screen) who is appearing in the corner of their field of vision as a pop up balloon.

During a presentation on parenting, the doctor and behavioural student Gabor Mate recited the content of a text exchange between his teenaged son and one of his friends, to illustrate the point of "being with" and how little content it really requires. This is an approximation:

A - ?

B - Yeah

A - ok

B - ok

A - lol

B - ha

A – yeah

B – (:

A – wut

B - ?

A – (smiley face)

B – (sad face)

A - ok

The point is that "being with" does not necessarily require content; it requires *being with*.

Ghost Buzzes have zapped into the path of the traditional glance around the room. Possibly because now there is so seldom anyone else in the room, but anyway, within a few months of carrying a cell phone most users feel a buzz, and jerk out their phone accordingly, when in fact there was no buzz. No message. No content in the feed.

What is a Ghost Buzz? The sense that someone else is thinking of you? The sense of obligation popping like a bubble on the surface of the consciousness of what one might have done?

"I was thinking about you…" is not a phrase one expects to hear in the instant messaging era. Because if one was thinking of another, they probably would have buzzed. If they didn't buzz, the assumption is, these days, that they were not thinking of you.

If I have 500 "friends" on facebook, which I actually do – because only my actual friends are admitted to my facebook – why don't I have more messages? Well, I had 500 friends before facebook, and I only ever heard from a few of them in any given week. And sometimes from none. And some of them I haven't seen or spoken to in years.

The feed, huh?. If one was a captive barnyard animal, one might be accustomed to a "feed" procedure, whereby at night and in the morning they could look forward to a resupply of their grain or straw or hay. Today human beings nudge a button and receive their feed. It comes from the same place; it is selected on the basis of what was last provided; it consists of an increasingly limited variety.

"My feed" may be determined by the last several google searches I entered.

So I am fed by whom? With what? And what hunger is being satiated? "Feed" in this case used to refer to a technological solution to providing audio/visual to another, ie, "live feed" meaning "connection" – not "food." Not content. Just the connection itself.

Of course people are fed by many things that they can get only by a mobile phone. But that relationship between the phone as the master's tool, and the possibility of those roles reversing, are intriguing.

Increased communication has been one of the heavyweight advances of the age of information. In Kenya, cell phones have basically made running obsolete. No one needs to run to the next village to confirm the market day or the products to be supplied. They just need to text. Construction of cell phone towers has out-paced the need to build roads, in some cases. In America, it has made anticipation and calculated expectation obsolete. If there is an issue, they will text me.

With 20% accuracy, people who have never met will decide to go on a date. Compare that to two people who have made eye contact, and observed each other, across a crowded room. This latter pair has an 80% chance of properly assessing the object of their admiration – without having exchanged a single word.

Digitally: *Yes, I like horses and reading magazines*; and, *yes, you like period drama and cooking*. I know more about my online date, but I also know a lot less.

People can feast on connections to others who are crazy about the same movies they are. Twi-Hards and Potter Heads are two distinct groups, with something of a rivalry going on out there in... cyberspace. Anonymous online chat rooms have sorted fans of werewolves and fans of sorcerers into two very distinct groups.

Is online gaming a feed? Is it social food? As one gamer talks to another by a real time audio transmitter, while blasting enemy images, until the sun comes up?

Family dinners are a kind of social legend, often marking important events and rattling or confirming the family dynamic when power and prestige are established over awkward silences or profusions of popularity. Hand held social media enabled devices, and the often, ahem, "unfiltered" posts now appearing direct from the dining room table are pushing the case of *Private v. Public* to new levels. Certainly there has been many a family dinner, extended family – at birthdays or seasonal gatherings – where most of the conversation took place quietly in muttered quips held back behind the voice box by that filter which separates appropriate from inappropriate statements. And whatever was said, appropriate, helpful, or otherwise, was unheard by anyone outside that dining room except as repeated gossip and was therefore muted to something quite second-hand and unreliable. Something non-binding.

These days the family fight over Christmas Dinner can be appreciated by everyone even in the outer circles of the facebook contingency. Occasionally in real time. Many family dinners are reduced by the staccato of typing - under the table – which is transliterating the unsaid comments to the digital world. From whence they will inevitably rebound to future family encounters. Brutal family arguments have been posted to facebook pages.

Sometimes family occasions are completely blotted out by the need, of some involved, to get on to more aesthetic views, whereby the participants can photograph themselves all jumping at the same time at some historic waypoint, and the commentary can be controlled by the typing, and then transmitted to select "friends." These choreographed moments then become the real legacy of the trans-continental trip, shared by many and understood to be the real highlight of the encounter. Except that many of the actual participants in the visit were not there, were not invited to be in the shot, were not invites on the road trip. The posts tell the story as the poster wishes it to be, just like any three versions of the same event would differ.

But the facebook version of life-as-we-want-it-to-appear means constantly posing for photos and posting while at a great place or at a special time or a great restaurant "having a super time." But this is "still life", or "life interrupted," or maybe "posed life." What actually happened was that the three teenage girls, or the two 20-somethings, were waiting in line outside a crowded restaurant where they… ate a late dinner without incident or intrigue. The picture they posted was of themselves letting out a single whoop while carefully positioned backwards against the neon sign of the restarant so bot they and the sign were in the frame.

People who post images of their breakfasts, their visits to great hotels, their face in front of worldly views: are they not bragging? If that image – worth a thousand words – was translated into actual conversation, what would be its social value? Never mind the two-hour slide-show from Aunt Agatha's trip to Denver; what do we call the everyday post of a dozen images from elsewhere?

Can it be described as insensitive to post a photo of

a brunch at a hotel most of your "friends" could never afford to eat at? Or is it an indication of the way we behave diferently around different people, who we value for different things. I wouldn't go on a socialist tirade with my high school friend – we would talk about our kids. I really care about her take on some of those things. But if I post my tirade, and she reads it, is she going to think I don't care about her?

The public posts on facebook cannot possibly be understood by all the Friends in the same way, just as no one would say the same kinds of things to all their different acquaintances. Many people pass remarks on facebook that they would never dream of uttering in the presence of their grandmothers, let alone to their grandmothers. What will the grandchildren of these many people hold back on account of respect?

Cyber-bullying betrays the presence of real power in these online spaces. A modern suite has been written, based on The Nutcracker, to help educate the young people through their experience: The facebook Suite, in six orchestral movements:

> The Dream of Friends
> The Ecstasy of Sharing
> Jig of the Bots
> Waltz of the Trolls
> Nightmare in All Caps
> In the Light of Day
> Auntie Media's Tea

Social media produces the sensation, or the impression, that one is informed, engaged, heard… but how would that be measured? By retweets? By likes? It will certainly not be measured and reaffirmed in person. Who recalls all the messages they thumbs-upped or thumbs-downed? Perhaps such computer-generated campaigns as that of Canadian Prime Minister Justin Trudeau will vindicate the social media participants. What will the others do?

Surveys are still conducted by companies who rely on a list of land-line phones. So those surveys will be vastly out of step with the surveys compiled by artificial intelligence collecting data from webpages. Who is the President? What if the digital nation and the analog nation are inclined to continue to disagree, and the difference in the way they communicate drives that gap deeper?

Social media is more than just a platform, and one of its many functions is also the new "411" phone directory.

But is the "social network" really working? And is it social? or is it basically overwhelmed? A person with anything to offer or gain would have to be online, on all 19 feeds, 24/7 in order for their online presence to be effective. Effective as people expect: ie, influential. Or, they could pay an ad agency for "#1 on Google!" presence.

The expectations of the accurate representation of

people and causes on social media is disappointed, and misunderstood. People expect exposure based on merit – but it works according to paid advertising. While it appears to be a social, and populist, theatre of interaction – it is just an enormous advertisement, peppered with real world, real time content provided at no charge by activist and employee users. There are a few vagaries in the question of *Paid v. Popular* circulation.

Basically, they are feeding us to ourselves. We provide the content and facebook, youtube and twitter sells it back to us for the price of the advertisements.

And what of art? And its appropriation by social media users? Who seldom even credit the artist, and never purport to represent the artist's card? How much is social media in control of what is considered art? When does everyone die of celebrity fatigue?

Pre-recorded entertainment, around here, seems to have competed successfully for social contact. Entertainment, preferably enjoyed at home, alone, seems to have relieved us of any risks attached with the benefits of interacting with others: we just watch and are not seen. We get to stare at someone's face for hours, get to know them. Home theaters and cheap digital livestream channel all manner of two dimensional human behaviour to the ruin of museums, art galleries; even the art of conversation.

And what happens when a person's eyes and ears,

heart and mind, become bloated on indigestibly synthetic choreographed drama? There must be some kind of outlet, some avenue for re-assessing what was taken in; some avenue for expression which does not require the now extinct venues of theatre, café, market or dance hall for expression? The same glowing tablet takes messages to the outside world – at least to the digital cyber space – even photos and videos. I can join a chat to discuss the TV series.

Social needs are real. When all avenues of access to meeting them have been ultimately rerouted, cut off or detoured, those needs are – strictly speaking – not being met. When all manner of socializing leads ultimately to a cluster of heads turned down to glowing tablets and thumb tapping, social needia's strangle hold on the deficiency syndrome can be seen. The fewer social needs are met in social environments, the more social needia.

Popping bubbles with "thumbs up" reply and presenting ideas which require less than 142 characters to articulate is not good social exercise. Someone Somewhere Else can be relied upon to "like" the momentary status of the human condition. Or swallow the bait and choke up some argument. But it is so disconnected from a human interaction, the results are just not going to be useful.

The need for social contact is not actually satisfied by text bubbles and hysterical textual arguments any more than it is satisfied by bullying or toadying or suffering victimization.

Great campaigns are marshalled by targetting "groups" vulnerable to "tags" with at least as much sophistication as if fish were being shot in a bucket. How? Those people actually then show up to events.

Social status was once connected with action in a person's world; in one's neighbourhood; in one's travels; in relationships like helping or leading or healing or teaching or growing food. Now people can invent their social role by staging selfies with unsuspecting – or too polite – real-world leaders and heroes. People get to curate themselves, posting their own contrived captions. And it never hurts to have a small army of fixers who work that facebook page 24/7 getting new "friends" and plying their feeds with compliments and sympathetic statements. Enough to guarantee that any little quip garners 900 "likes."

900 "likes" is cred. And these days, it's displayed right there on the screen next to the face. It's as if that head cheerleader, the one with a team of back up dancers and hero jocks wrapped around her finger on the football field, actually took them with her wherever her profile was invoked.

Facebook might better have been named maskbook. Its common usage defines it as a tool for people to design the face they show the world, edit it, airbrush it, link it to other popular faces, spin it. This privilege was previously reserved to politicians and the monarchy, using the mass media hounds and editors to cope with the job of narrowing the nose and capture exactly the right angle on baby kissing. No wonder Everyman has latched onto it.

But is it politicians or monarchy or celebrity whom the people wish to emulate? Or do they desire to live more fully in their own world, to be really really more themselves – bigger, better and more? To do more, think more, feel more, to beeeee more? To change or improve their world? Our own world is fraught with difference, shortcomings, need for cooperation, need for revolt: not so much the need for relief of celebrity fatigue in the form of making ourselves the (often disappointing) heroes behind our own online avatar. Because the revolution will still not be televised – because the revolution can only happen in city blocks, burroughs, rural roadblocks, And it can only happen where people are interacting and relying on each other - 100%.

People, especially activists, always used to resist surveillance and monitoring. Those activities used to be elaborate: used to require street intelligence to introduce and send actors in costumes to somewhat secret meetings. Now people, activists, have their contacts displayed publicly. They post statements that are perched on the border of incriminating, and leaning ponderously to the wrong side.

Now people who have never acted in any type of resistance, or protest capacity, post every thought that crosses their mind. People used to go into a church and then into the back and then into a small closet and speak quietly and maybe not fully to a priest about their confessions, while now they write them in great detail and post them publicly.

Does this technology herald a fundamental shift in human relations and social structure and the role of the individual and the group? Out in the village, a person gets to smile at who they like, shun who they don't, and even whisper gossip at anyone they particularly don't like. That happens in real time. It happens sometimes involuntarily, unexpectedly. That is real time.
Posing in real time is bizarre, it's not a winning act. Posing on facebook is encouraged. Will people remember how to behave when they go out in public? Will people contemplate the difference in their online and actual behaviours?

People didn't use to tell their most heartfelt moments, especially the ones they were most proud of or moved by, because those are private moments; because private moments can be used against a gal by people opposed to her; because emotional property, if you'll allow it, isn't usually shared with people who hate you.

How do you know there are people who hate you out there, making themselves your friend on facebook? The matter of surveillance is no longer up for discussion since Mark Zuckerburg met with the heads of Britain's and the United States of America's intelligence and security agencies, at their demand, and came out of it with the whole network functioning fully and unaltered, and the spies satisfied. A guy's new girlfriend discusses his ex-wife with her facebook friends and finds out enough to know she wears a wig (a tightly held secret), and then broadcasts that in the business end of a social blackmail procedure.

The first time I ever heard of facebook, I was stopping by on someone at her office. This was in 2004. She interrupted our conversation when something popped up on her screen and caught her attention, and she dealt with that right away. She then explained that someone had recently joined facebook and made "friend requests" of herself and several other facebook "friends." They didn't really want to be associated with her, but they weren't prepared to be so openly hostile as to deny her "friend request." So they all accepted the request, and then they adjusted the settings concerning that person so that she could only access pictures of their pets. Meanwhile, the not very good "friends" had full access to the newbie's page, posts and friends. And it gave them a lot of entertainment.

A hammer can be used to build a bridge, and a hammer can be used to knock a bridge down.

Social needs include affirmation, recognition, love, identity, and a sense of place. They also include limitation, correction, direction. These are things which are sometimes hard to accept, sometimes hard to really detect and appreciate and get used to. These are things which are often given subtly. These are the things which take time to stick in place, to calcify, maybe, and build backbone and independence and self-confidence. These are things which should be tested for resistance by real people – not bubbles. Bubbles don't really sink in the way a matriarch's expression of approval, or disapproval, does.

Online, where there are fewer matriarchs anyway, challenging notions can be easily dismissed with a click.

Very often, social need(ia)s reserve and eventually diminish themselves to images and videos of cats and dogs. "Vines" feature girls slipping off the hoods of cars; children talking back to their parents; and can one really express themself and their development in a video of a horse nodding along to a Top 40 song?

"Social" media is not very social at all. And the "media" in question is possibly the most limiting in the history of form. It is described in terms of gigabytes, but what everyone seems to have forgotten is that a gigabyte of data is a very tiny thing indeed.

A real, live person should play with someone their own size.

THE AUTONOMOUS NERVOUS SYSTEM

When you meet someone who you fall in love with, then their absence creates a vacuum where before there was nothing: the autonomous nervous system recognizes that something needs to be done. It picks up the reins and fastens on spurs.

Thank god for the autonomy of that nervous system. It is never to be reasoned with, or placated by any logic, explanation, reward for silence, treat, substitute or opiate; never to be scolded into submission by learned values; never to adjust its behavior based on past mistakes and failure. It can only be satisfied by the presence of that other, the person. The beloved.

That cosmic intelligence never acceded to rules of any kind. It has remained autonomous within the human body through a protracted evolutionary journey that every other function and form has adapted to out of necessity: run; fight; eat; get along; sleep; get a job; be responsible; be polite. Grow taller; store more fat; make the thigh bones slighter. The autonomous system only knows what the heart truly needs, the spiritual heart that was born for only one mission.

The sensibility and capability of that system is such to cause pain, anxiety, exhaustion when the other is gone; to supply the mind with constant advertisements of sweet relief in many forms which would be brought with closeness. The autonomous nervous system has never forgotten the truth of the spirit's cause.

The starry constellation of true spirit was cloaked in flesh and bone and behaviours in order to survive here, here in the playing field of the universal destiny. The autonomous nervous system remains as an axis – the seeing mountain at the center – unaffected and unburdened by the requirements of the physicality of this life, just defying physical threats. It pumps the heart and lungs; causes perspiration or shivering to regulate the temperature; it dulls pain when necessary; it breakers electricity through the brain; revives a dead body that has not completed its integral task. And it is alert for love.

The starry constellations of the ageless spirits who dressed up in bodies to enter this life are yearning to complete themselves, or to perfect themselves, or to save themselves from disharmony of the galaxies, whoever they are. The only way change can be made to a constellation – thousands of trillions of tons of space and sun and moon and rocky planet – is if another constellation comes close. Closer than possible under the physic laws of space and matter. But the magnetic gravity supplied by the other, another constellation, can extend the arms of a spiral system. Perhaps a moon is drifting off; perhaps a comet is coming too close. The other is needed. And the two which can balance each other become human beings in order to get close enough that the ecstasy of spinning draws all things into harmony – and then, as human beings, they find each other to be the only things that can calm a heartbeat, soothe a mind. And they spin.

The timeless legacy of stars itself cannot automatically shift. It cannot defy gravity itself. So the person is the manifestation of an entire constellation, an entire collection of galaxies, when it is trying to maintain its continuum against the vagueries of an infinite universe.by leaning on a parallel one; an inner one; an intuitive one. The beings intertwine, untangle, lift each other higher, let each other fly – and there, beyond the blackness of the sky above them, the attainment of their perfection is mirrored in the galactic heavens which breathe in that straight love and exhale into a relaxed position.

The autonomous nervous system found in human beings is an electromagnetic repeater of the center against which all the infinite details of time and space push and pull and turn.

Eventually, here, the individual finds another person whose simple presence can pull and push and ease the stars that swirl in the chest, just by its exact magnetism and complementary weight. The person has encountered the stars it was born to be saved by – dressed up in another body which it was born to save. When the other is gone too far away to help, the autonomous nervous system within the individual responds by giving distress signals. That is what falling in love is for, that is what is happening when we say, "I am falling in love," even though human beings have collectively, culturally, forgotten. Love is the code that speaks to the autonomous nervous system which was wired to find balance. The autonomous nervous system answers only to love – not the forgetful human cultures' demands. And love is not its master but its star-studded compass.

Love is a compass. When love is trained on another, the autonomous system drives to follow it and leads the body and the mind by creating a wall of unpleasant sensations in every other direction than the shortest distance to the Other. Nausea, sleeplessness, an inability to eat, mental anguish, chest pain, grief, the worst memories of loss, a sense of drowning: these all confront a person when they resist the course of love's guiding needle; when love has pointed and the feet do not march. When the heart is set on fire and the arms move for buckets of water to douse it. But no substance can quench love, nothing but the Beloved – which only satisfies the need but fuels the flames and encourages the burning down, the star-becoming.

In its autonomy, this nervous system has no allegiance to the human being – only to the spirit, to the entire cosmos. It is distinct and unsworn to social mores, decency, timeliness, embarrassment, and so on. It is not a servant of the body's individual comfort, only the starry constellations' needs. It will burn and blind the body that carries it if the body does not cooperate. Very dangerous for a fragile human.

Having no care for the individual fashioned by the proportions of the body and its talents or shortcomings, its place in society, the autonomous nervous system has famously led slaves and peasants to woo nobility. It has joined princes with farm girls; queens with knaves; prostitutes with Messiahs. The spiritual journey can only be made with the help of a deeper sense – one that cannot be conditioned or forget. Life is too hard, too fraught, to leave people in charge of their destinies. Hence the need for a system autonomous of the evolving body and the opinionated mind, yet within the starry constellation cloaked in meat.

And yet the meat has elemental rings through its tender nose, by which it may be led. And the mind has limits: it cannot conceive of forever, but it might be motivated by the thought of oblivion. The heart and the spleen and the liver and the lungs and kidneys produce their own emotions. And they can be inflamed or strangled of energy.

Physical desire is the big stick which the universe has provided for the autonomous nervous system to beat the body in the right direction. The sweetness of kissing, the will to caress and satiate. Transcendental bliss is a powerful motivator. And even if the body has never experienced it, the autonomous nervous system recalls, and plays tapes, and exposes the nerves to a taste. But only if the person falls in love.

Consider, the body can only experience pleasure in love. The mind only rests or ignites or pursues at the knowledge or prospect of love. The emotions sail best on love's breeze. The passions are charged by love. Every song that was ever made and remembered was a love song.

Other Big Sticks were given out selectively: to the poets,

the singers, the warriors, the playwrights, the musicians, the writers. Even to the scientists, the essential tool of persuasion was given (rationale), in order that the diversity of lovers might multiply and make possible every solution needed by the unfolding universes. The artists were given beauty and terrible truth; the engineers scope.

But humans, or some other force among them, have always contrived to cheat the Autonomous of these persuaders: calling on "religious purity" and emphasizing the pejorative of the cunning brain superior to the body's physical drives and longings; the heart's ease; the spirit's sigh. At other times the contrary forces defy science and heroism, depending on the lovesick target of their destructive ways. Organization among people, just to allow bodies to survive more comfortably, or to allow some bodies to live richly on the work of other bodies, has skewed spiritual journeys. Although every poet warns of the urgency to heed love, and sentinels love's reward, sometimes duty to the physical body's survival, or to the ego, or to comfort, is confused with importance. Sometimes desire is not enough. Sometimes the rewards are so unfamiliar as to strain credulity.

If a human being does not give in to the desire for pleasure, it may give in to pain. Melancholy is a choice tool among stars who wish to expand, to swirl more gracefully. And the Autonomous administers it in order to maneuver the representative body in the only possible direction for relief; the only possible direction to ensure the stars will continue to turn. But the emotions can be sedated with drugs by those who would suffer for the individual's vagrancy. They can become addicted to themselves, even, in belligerence or the absence of cultural learning.

Sometimes desire can be deliberately, cunningly redirected at a false target by outside hands. People have been drugged or cast spells upon; seduced or lied to in ways that make them attach to another and break the Beloved's heart. Sometimes the institution of monogamy has barred heavenly peace. Sometimes it is the institution of religion, and opposing religions, and deeply indoctrinated fears of afterlife reprisal for betrayal of "god" by engagement of "the infidel." Sometimes it's the economy.

Not to worry. Soon after the beloved is encountered, a person is subject to purification by lovesickness. Self-doubt projects every shortcoming, every unworthy act ever committed and every dubious belief which might jeopardize union on the inside of the forehead. A fever of terror grips the body and it sweats as if in a ceremony or a trial. What can be done? Fear of inadequacy launches a thorough cleansing of bad habits until the whole system has been laundered – whether through penance, promise or at least recognition. Often by the total capitulation of the human being's governing structure: faiths can be abandoned. The human being has been forced to recognize the importance of being worthy of the Other, lest nightmares come to rule.

One might find herself unable to do anything but lay

in bed, actively lay in bed and concentrate on the light they saw emanating from the Other; imagine bathing herself in it; allow the glowing radiation to enter the chest and watch as black clots of trapped, dead emotional blood ooze away from the heart. She might witness her own heart, pulsating and renewing in pink mists flecked with gold and white light. One might look up in detachment as a rusty jail door swings open out the rib cage, might see the back of an old bear walking away from a long imprisonment – walking away but not hurrying, not even looking back, just deciding on freedom after a long retreat in hibernation. The door was never locked. One might detect a substance like fishing line caught tightly in and around the ribs, knot upon knot upon snared tangle tightening the chest wall and cutting into the heart and vertebrae, pulling tighter with each breath, forbidding love. One might feel the knots loosen or dissolve.

One might turn back around and visualize pulling thorns from the beloved's skin and soothing the nettle stings of rejection and loss with salve of adoration. One might pour the precious salve of love - not knowing if his own heart reaches hers or only the other way round: very biologically expensive. Love is unconditional. Now and then it is only necessary for one to love the other, because the act of love is itself the adjustment that is needed; the purification will happen regardless of mutuality.

There is, however, no lasting cure for lovesickness but the beloved. Particularly devastating in the unrequited form. People don't die from the drugs and medications which unenlightened doctors prescribe for the moodiness, irrational pain and headaches. People don't die from self-medication. People die from the lovesickness; from the absence. They die because they did not offer the beloved what it needed. They were not able to offer themselves entirely.

The autonomous nervous system is an encryption of the spiral itself. The spiraling stars have billions of years to grow and shift, yet they may have only one lifetime among many to move in a single form and merge with the Other in that proxy tangent. Generations overlap. If one life refuses, another must replace it. The autonomous nervous system can kill. It is not embedded in the individual for the sake of the individual.

The autonomous nervous system will threaten the physical body with death if it will not carry itself into union with the essential Other. Insomnia, high blood pressure, wasting, addiction to substances, mindlessness, can all be fatal.

The sensual stream of potential: the images and sensations sent to the brain, the breast, the fingers and lips and eyes and ears, would sabotage any hunter or diver; any speaker or negotiator. Delirium in the form of intrusive thoughts – if longing to manifest the thoughts cannot win out – would kill any active person, or maybe cause an inactive one to be fired from their job.

The hallucinations: seeing the beloved around every corner, at every gate, in every cloud, in every crowd, could make a person lose their friends. Love has abandoned living bodies to miserable fates of decades of servitude and insanity when the individual refused it.

The endless universe cheats space by allowing the spiral galaxies to inhabit living beings capable of dancing hand in hand with another. And it cheats time by allowing them to appear and reappear throughout history, to make adjustments one by one. When you fall in love, the Other's stars show themselves even in the daylight; even under a roof. While the eyes can no longer understand, they still see. They still recognize.

Stars show themselves in the eyes. Scientists have taken pictures of the iris and put them next to pictures of the cosmos. They are identical. When lovers meet, the stars come out. When people make love while staring into each other's eyes, the stars turn between them. The universes lay themselves out and intertwine and untangle.

We are these people, and we know this to be true.

We are pulling each other through time when we give in to love's current. Love forges and designs families, countries, continents: why not the universes; why not the stars themselves?
What else would the astrologers have to say to us, if they couldn't see the collision courses between people and advise action on account of the two strata of stars? That's why we have astrologers, they are counseling against fates not worth having, and they are seers of love at work. They help bring us together.

Such a dangerous calling. A fragile body. A mind

vulnerable to madness. The stars risk it all on us, just to keep shining. We say we risk everything for love, but there is nothing to risk but losing love. What would a person risk? Their loneliness? Forty years of suffering? "Ah, yes! I am going to put my loneliness right there on the table, *it's winner take all*!" Be driven by love. It points true.

If love was denied, would anything else survive?

Children come of love. They carry the fate of us all, past and future, and they must love: they must allow the stars to keep spinning gracefully, to keep twinkling. Unless when we see a shooting star it is not actually dying but… moving. Or it is a life given up on by love, soon to be replaced.

Imagine dying, returning to the stars, only to see the Beloved streak past in a blaze of dying light. Imagine watching the Beloved go out. And heed that pain – prevent it from ever happening. And keep in mind that love works both ways.

Pain is the master now. Leave him. Run.